The Outcome Generation

How a New Generation of Technology Vendors Thrives Through True Customer Success

RED RAVEN BOOKS

Publisher: The Copy Collective Pty Ltd, Suite 317, 185 Elizabeth St, Sydney NSW 2000, Australia

Copyright © Paul J Henderson

National Library of Australia Cataloguing-in-Publication Data. A catalogue record for this book is available on request from the National Library of Australia.

Book Layout © The Copy Collective Pty Ltd

Printed and bound by IngramSpark

ISBN 978-0-6482161-0-0

Generation 3 Customer Success is documented common sense—and it makes sense. It can be implemented simply or can be the foundation to drive a deep customer success culture.
Ronnie Altit, Chief Executive Officer, Insentra Group

Paul has managed to distil much of what we now think we know about customer success and how critical it is to vendor success. This should be required learning for aspiring sales leaders so they can deliver better outcomes.
Mark Pretty, Managing Partner Global Technology, Odgers Berndtson

Subscription pricing and recurring revenue are changing the technology landscape. The power has moved back to customers. If customers don't feel successful, the vendor's revenue suffers. Paul shows vendors how to turn this change to their advantage.
Matthew Michalewicz, CEO, Complexica

Customer success outcomes are proven and easy to implement. We've used the approach (with a different name) for five-plus years, with great financial results (highest services profitability ever) and high customer satisfaction.
Peace Chen, VP Asia Pacific Services, QAD

This is a timely book that illustrates how a customer's success is intrinsic to a vendor's success. Paul unpacks a best-practice framework for achieving benefit in an evolving field.
Daniel Pettman, CIO, BaptistCare

I had the privilege of working with Paul for five years, during which the program outlined in the book was employed. This business-results and outcomes-based customer engagement approach echoes very well with both existing and new customers.
Jay Cao, VP Greater China, QAD

TABLE OF CONTENTS

INTRODUCTION

The CEO of the marketing-automation vendor called a crisis meeting. Their largest customer had threatened to cancel their contract. The CEO opened the meeting, *'Tell me what's happened.'*

The VP of Services said:

Our system is a great fit for their Marketing needs. We've trained their Marketing team well, and they love the system. They're using it perfectly. They've created a stream of new leads which they've passed to Sales. The problem is simple—Sales hasn't closed the leads. And that isn't our problem. We've done our job by helping them create leads.

The CEO said:

And yet they're planning to cancel our contract. And that makes it our problem. Tell me, what was the business case they used when they decided to subscribe to our system? What outcome would we help them achieve?

The VP of Sales said:

They want to increase sales. They want 40% of sales revenue to come from marketing-created leads. And that hasn't happened. Regardless of whose fault it is, top management feel something must change. They're considering an outside lead-generation firm to create their pipeline, so they won't need us. Our problem is Sales feel the leads Marketing passes over aren't qualified. So,

1

Sales isn't following them up. Marketing insists they've qualified the leads.

The CEO said:

Sounds like the problem lies in the transition from Marketing to Sales.

We'd better get someone to investigate and find an answer.

The vendor was fortunate. They had a consultant whose background included both sales and marketing. The consultant knew how the end-to-end process should work. The consultant helped the customer put a service level agreement in place between Marketing and Sales. The agreement defined when leads should be passed to Sales, and what would then happen. Technically, this work was outside the vendor's normal scope. But the customer was happy to pay for the consulting. And it worked. Sales started to get leads they knew were ready for their involvement. So, they chased them and closed them.

The vendor had learned a tough lesson. It wasn't enough to focus on the direct benefit of using their system—creating leads. They needed to focus on the outcome the top management of a customer would regard as a success. If they didn't, their revenue would suffer.

They're not the only vendor to learn that lesson. There's a new generation of technology vendors. They've developed absolute clarity about what the top management of their customers consider success to be. And they've built their business around enabling that success. They know the only thing that matters is the outcome the customers achieve. These vendors are all members of the Outcome Generation.

This book provides a pragmatic framework for vendors to join the Outcome Generation. It describes how members of the Outcome Generation work. And it then offers a six-step program for implementing a true customer success program—one that enables an outcome top management of the customers regard as success.

It starts with defining that success—called a success outcome. A success outcome is an ongoing business result that top management of the customer regard as success. And for which the vendor is the primary external provider.

The book then introduces a framework for developing a customer success program unique to the vendor. The DEEP framework describes the four phases of engagement with customers in the Outcome Generation—Develop, Evaluate, Execute and Prosper. Using the four phases, the vendor defines a lifecycle with ideal customers and the deliverables from each lifecycle step.

Next, the vendor analyses their execution capability—their capability to put in place the lifecycle they've decided to pursue.

The execution capability analysis becomes a key input for an implementation plan. And this in turn drives the staged rollout of the customer success program.

Finally, there's growth through new products and services. The lens of the success outcome helps generate innovative growth ideas and drive loyal revenue growth for the vendor.

Paul Henderson learned the lessons that led to this six-step program first-hand. He spent over five years designing and running customer success programs across Asia Pacific. Before dedicating himself to writing this book, Paul ran the Asia Pacific region for an enterprise software company. He led 200 professionals in nine countries supporting 800 enterprise customers.

The business competed with the largest software companies. These competitors had more resources and much greater market recognition. They were also recommended by the large consulting firms (who had implementation teams they wanted to keep busy). Lots of smaller companies also competed in the market, often on price. It was a tough competitive market. But most vendors in the technology space face tough competition.

So, Paul considered how he could develop new growth ideas and differentiate from the competition. He decided to pursue an outcomes-based approach. He and his team focused on delivering real and measurable business outcomes for customers. Not just getting the software live, but real business results.

He also examined the bigger outcome his customers wanted to achieve—the success outcome (although he didn't have that label at the time). He realised customers bought ERP software to achieve effective operations. He realised he could do much more of what the customer needed to achieve effective operations. Which he and his team did.

Paul developed a strong belief that technology vendors should enable outcomes the top management of customers consider to be success. Getting IT systems live was necessary, but not enough. The vendor should understand everything the customer must do to achieve their success outcome. And help with most of it. He also realised that enabling the customer's success outcome helped the vendor thrive—to enjoy loyal revenue growth.

Paul realised his experience could help other organisations. So, he left the software company to research and then write this book. It's based on his experience in leading customer success programs for over five years and on more than a year of research since.

His sincere hope is that it will help other vendors enjoy the benefits of joining the Outcome Generation.

PART 1
THE OUTCOME GENERATION AND CUSTOMER SUCCESS

Technology vendors have always tried to enable customer success. But the definition of customer success has changed.

Traditional vendors have focused on the direct benefits from use of their products or services. But customers buy technology products and services as a means to an end—to achieving a bigger outcome. Vendors need to enable that bigger outcome.

In the past, vendors haven't had a lot of financial incentive to ensure their customers' success. Subscription pricing changes everything. There's now a financial imperative to invest in customer success.

Technology vendors want to grow revenue, differentiate from competition and generate new ideas for growth. Generation 3 Customer Success helps in all three areas.

Customer Success programs can deliver strong financial returns.

There's been an explosion of interest in customer success, and its corollary, delivering business outcomes. Here's what industry leaders say:

Nothing is more important to Salesforce than customer success...
Marc Benioff, CEO, Salesforce (Evans, 2017)

Our sense of purpose lies in our customers' success.
Satya Nadella, CEO, Microsoft (Evans, 2017)

But what we're going to do is put a little more focus on customer success, so that we're capturing and documenting and codifying the business value that gets created, which helps a CIO or an IT department within their organization demonstrate the value they are driving inside their company and frankly helps us on upsells, on price realization and on landing new accounts.
John Donahoe, CEO, ServiceNow (Evans, 2017)

If you stay very focused on customers and customer success, people pay attention to that—and in turn, they also want that same type of success.
Aneel Bhusri, CEO, Workday (Evans, 2017)

Today, when companies are buying a service [context is Software as a Service], they're buying an outcome.
Mark Hurd, CEO, Oracle (Dasteel, 2016)

Every business in the world needs to be thinking about customer success.
Clara Shih, Founder and CEO, Hearsay Social (Evans, 2017)

One of the foundations of our success at Salesforce was customer success.
Jim Steele, President and Chief Customer Officer, InsideSales, former President and Chief Customer Officer, Salesforce (Mehta, 2016)

The ability to succeed in this new economy will depend on how well you sell and deliver measurable business outcomes to your customers.
Jeb Dasteel, SVP and Chief Customer Officer, Oracle, et al (Dasteel, 2016)

...especially in the world of the Cloud, customer success is, it is the do or die.
Steve Lucas, CEO, Marketo (Planhat, 2017)

What is Customer Success?

These industry powerhouses make one thing certain. Customer success is now a central focus for the technology industry. But hasn't this always been the case? Haven't vendors always wanted their customers to be successful? And don't most vendors have customers who will attest to their success?

The answer to each question is 'yes'. Vendors have tried to deliver customer success. But the definition of customer success has evolved. Established, more traditional vendors talk of customers successfully using their products and services. And that makes sense. Customers should get a direct benefit from the products and services they buy. We hear the word 'value' a lot.

But there's an emerging understanding that delivering a direct benefit or value from a product or service isn't enough. Necessary, yes, but not enough. Customers buy technology products and services to achieve an end outcome. That end outcome isn't successful use of the product. Successful use of the product is a means to a bigger end outcome.

Success comes for a customer when they achieve that bigger outcome. A customer success program should focus on enabling that bigger outcome. And if the vendor can enable this bigger outcome, customer loyalty and revenue will soar.

As vendors, we want both loyalty and revenue growth. This book provides a path to these results—to loyal revenue growth.

The Old Attitude Towards Customer Success

There's vested interest for traditional vendors to deliver success for their customers. They want customers to pay maintenance; they hope to sell them more products and services; they need references for future selling. But most vendors just want their customers to have success from their products or services. That feels good.

In the past, the financial incentive to ensure customer success wasn't great. The bulk of revenue from a customer occurred early in the engagement. The customer bought perpetual licences upfront. And vendors offered discounts for them to buy all the licences they might need for the foreseeable future. The customers bought infrastructure such as servers upfront. The bulk of professional services were for implementation which happened upfront.

By the time the implementation was finished, the vendor had a big percentage of the revenue they would get from the customer over the next five years. Of course, maintenance revenue was important. But if customers continued using the software, they felt obliged to pay maintenance in case something went wrong. So, most customers paid their maintenance every year.

Occasionally, the vendor could sell add-on products and related services. Major upgrades took place from time to time but could often be years away. All in all, after the implementation there wasn't a lot of revenue on the horizon.

The vendor needed some customers to be successful because they needed references. References provide a powerful tool for the vendor sales team. But vendors didn't need all or even most of their customers to be successful. They needed enough to have references for the next sales deal.

As a result, if a customer wasn't successful, there wasn't a big financial downside for the vendor. Unhappy customers would usually feel their financial commitment was too large to drop the vendor. For most customers, it would be many years before they felt their initial investment was distant enough to throw out a vendor and start again.

The financial risk in a project lay with the customer. Vendors did what they could for customer success, but they weren't driven. It wasn't that they didn't care. It was just hard to find the financial reason for going the extra mile and ensuring the customer achieved the outcomes they wanted. There wasn't enough money in it.

This affected implementation projects. Everyone celebrated success when the software went live. In most cases, the vendor closed the project as soon as possible after go-live. For fixed-price projects, project closure was the final milestone affecting revenue recognition. Getting the project closed at the end of a quarter meant recognising the revenue in that quarter. It mattered. No-one wanted to keep the project open to measure the outcome from the project, particularly as reliable measurement could be three to twelve months into the future.

Everyone, including the customer, considered the project finished on go-live. No-one wanted to measure the results in case they weren't good. The customer's project team was often complicit. They had announced success with the go-live and didn't want measurement of real outcomes to change that perception of success.

Subscription Pricing Changes Everything

Things have changed for technology vendors. Now every vendor has a subscription pricing strategy. And that increases the need for customer success.

The revenue stream from a customer flows differently. When a customer chooses subscription pricing, the licence and infrastructure costs are spread over time. Many vendors are bundling implementation services and spreading that over time as well. The customer invests much less upfront.

After one or two years if things aren't going well, it's more palatable to drop the vendor and start again. Of course, it's disruptive to change vendors. The internal cost of a second implementation remains high and would not be done lightly. But the subscription fees wouldn't change much with the new vendor, so there's not a big direct impact on the P&L from this source.

The power pendulum has swung back in favour of the customer. They don't buy everything upfront. They invest over time. And they no longer bear the bulk of the risk for success. The following chart, reproduced from *Competing for Customers* (Dasteel, 2016), illustrates the change.

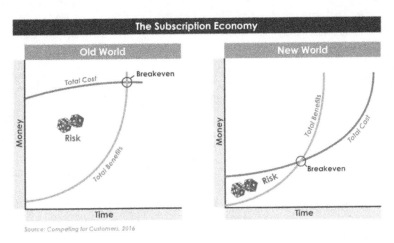

Fig 1: *Cost and benefit in the subscription economy*

Now the vendors' revenue streams have far more risk. The vendors have a much greater financial incentive to ensure customer success.

And customers are engaging with vendors differently. Paul Keen, CIO of Airtasker (an online marketplace for everyday tasks), said:

We try to have Tinder-style dates. If it works, we go ahead. If not, we stop. We may even use it for a period of time and then stop. Older vendors struggle with this concept. Newer vendors all understand this approach. And they work hard to ensure we have success.

The risk for vendors isn't only about being dropped. In fact, this represents the smaller of the risks from lack of customer success. The larger risk is lack of growth in usage.

To illustrate, let's assume a customer thinks they'll need 100 users, but only need 60 to start with. In the past with perpetual licences, the vendor would offer enough discount for the customer to buy all 100 upfront. With subscription pricing, customers rarely buy all users upfront. They're more likely to contract for 60 upfront and promise to buy more as usage expands. If they aren't successful, the use of the vendor's product won't increase, and the vendor won't sell any more users. Worse still, the customer's usage might decline, and the customer might cancel some of the original 60 users.

If the customers aren't successful, vendors now face the twin problems of increased risk of being dropped and reduced revenue growth. And that's why there's been an explosion of interest in customer success programs.

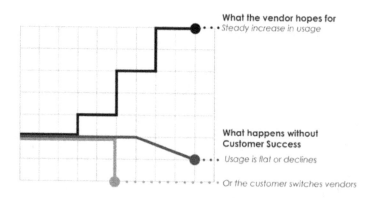

Fig 2: Potential revenue lost if customer doesn't succeed

Other Challenges for Technology Vendors

Growth

Vendors grow through cross-sell and upsell of existing products. They also want to grow from new products and services. The challenge is developing new offerings that will drive greater growth. It's not hard to generate lots of ideas. But how does a vendor generate ideas that will create real growth? What frame of reference can they use? And how do vendors make sensible decisions about which ones to choose?

Differentiation

Most vendors have competitors. Good competitors. The technology space is a tough market. It's difficult for most vendors to offer genuine product differentiation. If they do introduce new features, the competition will catch up fast. And then go past with something new of their own. Feature/function leapfrog is a never-ending game that becomes even tougher as products mature.

For services vendors, the challenge is even harder. They often develop small applications or add-ons to major applications, and that can help them differentiate. But for core services, it's hard for most customers to see much difference between the offering of one services provider and another.

Customer References — Advocates

It's extraordinarily hard to sell products and services without reference accounts. Most vendors have some friendly customers willing to take a reference call or host a reference visit. However, an analysis of the percentage of customers who are true reference accounts can produce a nasty surprise for many vendors.

And how many customers are true advocates? How many would proactively endorse a vendor's products or services? There's a big difference between a passive reference account that will take a call when asked and a proactive advocate spreading positive news.

Another problem has emerged for vendors. It's not difficult for prospects to find a vendor's customers. The prospects don't always ask the vendor for references. They often do their own checking. The vendor loses control of who the prospect talks with.

Is a Customer Success Program Cost-effective?

In the nascent world of customer success programs, vendors have implemented many different models. Some have separate customer success teams. Some of these see customer success and sales as different activities, others see them overlapping. Some customer success teams have responsibility for revenue, others don't. Other vendors see customer success as pervasive—as affecting every customer-facing department.

Regardless of the model, all share an underlying belief—they're financially better off having a customer success program. Let's explore where this financial benefit comes from.

We'll use a hypothetical vendor with:

- $100m of recurring revenue from current contracts and
- $25m of new customer sales each year (to organisations with whom the vendor has no prior relationship)

We'll consider three potential increases in revenue from a customer success program. And we'll calculate the three year returns as the compounding effect of recurring revenue is substantial.

Reduction in Churn

The first source of revenue is reduction of churn (loss of or reduction in the value of existing contracts). Basic customer success programs achieve churn reduction by monitoring customer usage and taking pro-active action. At the simplest level, they track how many of the licensed users are active. At a more advanced level, they track use of advanced features. This acts as a lead indicator of under-usage by a customer.

Vendors don't wait for the customer to tell the vendor they're cancelling—they look for early-warning signals and act immediately. This can have a big effect on discretionary churn. It's a great first step.

To illustrate the value of reducing churn, let's start with 4% churn and reduce it to 3%.

The Cumulative Cost of Churn		
Beginning Value of Contracts - $100m a year		
At End of Year	Value of these Contracts after 4% Churn	Value of these Contracts after 3% Churn
1	96	97
2	92.2	94.1
3	88.5	91.3
Total	276.7	282.4
Additional Revenue Over Three Years 5.7m		

Fig 3: The cumulative cost of churn

Each 1% of churn costs this vendor $1m in the first year. The compounding effect makes it $5.7m over three years.

Increased Upsell and Cross-sell

The second increase in revenue comes from increasing upsell (more revenue from existing customers on products/services they already use) and cross-sell (additional products and services to existing customers). A customer success program will accelerate acceptance of a vendor's offering. Tracking usage, both active users and key features, helps identify opportunities for both upsell and cross-sell. Operating in the Cloud gives vendors much greater insight into how customers use their products. They use this insight to drive pro-active action to increase upsell and cross-sell revenue.

An increase in upsell and/or cross-sell of 2% on the current recurring revenue of $100m would deliver $2m revenue in year one. The compounding effect makes it $12.1m over three years. This doesn't take account of churn (which would reduce the amount) and of new business sales (which would increase the size of the recurring revenue pool and thus increase upsell and cross-sell opportunities).

Improved New Customer Win Rates

The third revenue increase comes from improved new customer win rates. Our hypothetical vendor has $25m in new customer sales. Let's assume they have a 20% win-rate. They need to compete for $125m of business to win this $25m. If they could improve their win rate from 20% to 22%, they'd add $2.5m per annum or $7.5m over three years.

To summarise the results for our hypothetical vendor. They have $100m of recurring contracts at the start of the analysis. And they sell $25m of new contracts each year. With the small improvements set out above, they'd add the following revenue over three years:

Revenue Improvement	Amount
Reduction in churn of 1%	$5.7m
Increased upsell/cross-sell of 2%	$12.1m
Improved new customer win rate	$7.5m
Total	**$25.3m**

Fig 4: Potential additional revenue

In other words, on top of the growth already being achieved by this vendor, customer success would add $25.3m over three years.

Of course, achieving this $25m increase in revenue will incur additional cost. New staff, training, marketing materials and programs, new systems and management time and focus will all be needed. The cost will vary by vendor, and each will have a different hurdle for return on investment.

Simply put, there's substantial revenue available from implementing a customer success program.

Generation 3 Customer Success will eclipse Generation 2 in the same way that Generation 2 eclipsed Generation 1 in the early 1990s.

Organisations go through three logical steps (the logic chain) before they invest in technology. They decide their business results aren't adequate, they identify the problems and finally they identify requirements.

Generation 1 (Features Generation) vendors concentrated on the third step in this logic chain—meeting the customer's requirements.

Generation 2 (Solution Generation) vendors moved one step up the logic chain—solving the customers' problems.

Generation 3 (Outcome Generation) vendors move one step further up the logic chain—enabling future results.

Buying Technology Products and Services — The Logic Chain

Companies go through three logical steps (the logic chain) before they invest in technology. Before these steps begin, an event causes someone in the company to look at results. It may be budgeting, or an external event, or a regulatory change. But management focuses on results.

This leads to the first step in the logic chain. The company decides the results aren't good enough. Revenue may be too low, costs may be too high, the pipeline may be inadequate. They resolve to act.

Second, the company identifies the problems or roadblocks causing the inadequate results.

Finally, they'll come up with ideas for how to fix the problems. These ideas drive their requirements. Then they talk to vendors.

Fig 5: The logic chain

Vendors have always wanted their customers to be successful. The following chapters review the three generations of how vendors tried to make that happen.

Generation 1 – The Features Generation

Generation 1 vendors concentrated on the third step in the logic chain. They showed customers how they could meet the specified requirements.

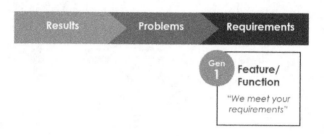

Fig 6: Generation 1

Generation 1 began in the '70s, a little after software packages appeared. Most technology vendors began by developing products or services for individual customers. After doing this with several customers, the vendors realised they couldn't sustain this development approach. They started to add features and functions to sell their offering to a broader market.

They soon realised they couldn't come up with products and services in isolation. The old adage of 'build it and they will come' just didn't work. They needed to understand their market and the specific wants and needs of the customers. So, they went to a great deal of trouble to learn the customers' wants and needs. Listening to the 'voice of the customer' became popular as a driver of marketing behaviour.

Generation 1 vendors then developed features and functions to match the customers' wants and needs. They believed the vendor that best matched the customers' wants and needs would win.

Competing for new business required lengthy demonstrations of features and functions of the software. External consulting organisations became adept at selling independent evaluation methodologies. Customers would engage the consultants to assist in determining which vendor had the closest fit to the requirements. Big spreadsheets with long lists of required features were common, with each vendor scored on each feature.

The term 'column fodder' appeared. Many customers needed to have three or more vendors ranked. Often the customer or the independent external consultant favoured one vendor. The requirements would favour that vendor. The other vendors were only there to provide scores in the other columns—they were the column fodder.

Problems arose on the customer side as well. The customer often included requirements far more advanced than they could use. The problem of internal people or consultants favouring one vendor made objective assessment difficult. As evaluations proceeded, the customers struggled to sort out what was important.

The Generation 1 era also saw a patchy approach to implementations. Vendors did not have robust implementation methodologies. The approach to implementation depended on the skill of the vendor's consultants. Each implementation was different, driven by the consultant's knowledge and biases. Measurement of results proved difficult. This may have led to the culture of declaring victory when the software was live, with no real attempt to measure the returns.

As the technology industry matured, the differences between software packages reduced. It became more and more difficult to differentiate. Customers needed to go into more and more detail to decide between vendors. The external consultants encouraged this drawn-out analysis. The cost for the vendor in running the sales campaign kept increasing, with the result often a lottery.

As the offerings became more similar, the customers had more difficulty remembering the features offered by each vendor. Conversations like the following occurred—'Which vendor had that feature we liked? Was it the one with the good sandwiches for lunch? I can't remember.'

Another problem then emerged—the customer didn't always know best. The customers had a limited view of how problems were solved in other companies. Vendors began to have broader experience and could apply lessons learnt in one customer to other customers.

Not surprisingly, vendors sought a new way to compete.

Generation 2 – The Solution Generation

Generation 2 vendors emerged in the late 1980s. They focused one step back up the logic chain. They no longer focused only on the customer's stated requirements. They worked to understand the customer's problems and then develop a solution. They told customers they needed first-hand knowledge of the problems. They'd then use their experience to come up with better solutions to solve them.

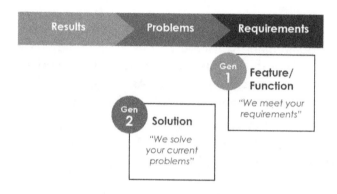

Fig 7: Generation 2

Solution-selling emerged. Lots of variations of solution selling appeared over the years. Each claimed superiority over its predecessors. But they all had one thing in common—they emphasised understanding the customer's problems and then providing a solution to those problems.

Generation 2 vendors did not compete on features and functions alone. They could compete on who could provide the best solution to the customer's problems. This brought into play other factors such as expertise and experience. Consultants in the sales team shifted from being experts in features and functions to experts on how to solve problems.

The solution-selling approach produced great results for vendors. Today, few vendors would choose a Generation 1 approach. The exception is those vendors who sell to government and other regulated bodies which insist on a Generation 1 approach.

Generation 2 also saw the quality of implementation methodologies improve. Each vendor had their own methodology, as did many consulting firms. In theory, every implementation would follow the same process. In practice, that didn't occur. But even a modicum of structured process improved the results.

Why Change from Generation 2?

Generation 2 has served the technology industry well for almost 30 years, with good reason—it worked. But Generation 2 vendors face some challenges.

Pace of Change

The pace of change in business has exploded. Technology has been the major driver of this acceleration. But other innovations such as the share economy and the subscription economy have changed businesses. This increasing pace of change makes it difficult for customers to stay ahead. If the customers and technology vendors focus on solving today's problems, they'll always be in catch-up mode. It takes a long time for customers to diagnose the current problems, agree requirements, choose a vendor and implement a solution. By that time, a whole new set of problems will have emerged. The customers will never get ahead.

The pace of change in business has been the largest factor driving a move from Generation 2. But it's not the only one.

Current-Solution Blindness

Customers suffer from 'current-solution blindness'. They have difficulty seeing solutions to their problems that differ much from the current method. The catch-cry of 'We've always done it that way' is common. As a result, it's difficult for them to come up with creative solutions they can ask their suppliers to meet. And it's difficult for them to see how an innovative offering from a supplier would work, or why they would bother making so much change.

Forbes contributors David Sturt and Todd Nordstrom said (Sturt, 2014):

> When it comes to creativity and innovation, customers can be woefully inadequate sources for new solutions. Inventors of market-disrupting ideas know that what people think will attract them to a new product or service may often be very different from what actually does.

In his book, serial entrepreneur Mark Cuban put it this way: Your customers can tell you the things that are broken and how they want to be made happy. Listen to them. Make them happy. But don't rely on them to create the future road map for your product or service. That's your job.

Or, as Steve Jobs famously put it: It's really hard to design products by focus groups. A lot of times, people don't know what they want until you show it to them.

When the pace of business change was more languid, current-solution blindness wasn't much of a problem. Today, businesses can be disrupted overnight. Business can't afford to be 'stuck in a rut'.

And current-solution blindness can affect vendors as well. When focusing on current problems, there's a tendency to start with the current offering. The easiest thing to do is tweak a current offering to overcome the problems. It's faster and cheaper. The result is small incremental changes over time.

Tweaking current products does two things. First, it tends to make software code complex. The term spaghetti code is often used to describe software that has evolved over time. It's hard to understand and difficult to maintain. Second, current-solution blindness stops vendors applying significant creativity to the customer's problems.

Vendors Only Focusing on Problems Is Like Doctors Only Treating Symptoms

Let's draw an analogy with the medical world, which has come a long way in the past 30 years. One of the developments has been the Patient Outcome Framework.

If a patient is unwell, they will explain their problems to the doctor. The doctor doesn't then prescribe treatment. The doctor uses the information about the patient to develop a diagnosis. They may need to do further tests before they finalise the diagnosis. They then develop a specific outcome to be achieved for that patient. For example, if the problem is cancer, the outcome will be to kill a particular type of tumour in a specific part of the body. That outcome is part of a bigger outcome of restoring health.

Only after defining a patient outcome does the physician determine the right treatment. In the case of, say, oncology, it might be radiotherapy, chemotherapy, surgery or a combination. In all cases, the doctors have an outcome to achieve for the patient. They then tailor the treatment to achieve the outcome.

This approach in medicine is world-wide. Most developed countries use a Patient Outcome Framework to ensure a focus on patient outcomes.

Customer problems are a lot like symptoms in the medical world. We now realise we must shift the focus from solving problems to delivering a clear business outcome. We can't concentrate on solving problems without being clear about the broader outcome. That's a lot like doctors giving medication to treat symptoms without first having a clear patient outcome to achieve.

We now understand technology vendors that don't focus on business outcomes are like doctors who don't focus on patient outcomes.

Fig 8: Medical professionals focus on patient outcomes

For subscription-pricing vendors, Generation 2 engagement does not produce the customer success needed to protect and grow recurring revenue. Generation 2 was adequate when most of the revenue came early in the relationship. With subscription revenue now spread over time and an increased ability for customers to drop vendors, Generation 2 just doesn't cut it.

Generation 3 — The Outcome Generation

Generation 3 vendors move the final step back up the logic chain. They focus on the future results or outcomes the customer wants to achieve. Their offering enables achievement of that future outcome. And the solution of current problems as a by-product.

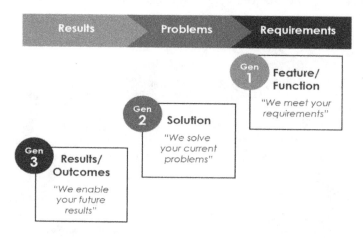

Fig 9: Generation 3

By focusing on future results, customers have a chance to get ahead. Instead of reacting to current business problems, they focus on what's ahead of them. And they want vendors who can help them get there. Perhaps even lead them there.

To be clear, Generation 3 vendors don't ignore the requirements or current problems. The customers want vendors to listen to them. They'll only listen to the vendors once they're sure the vendors have listened to them. But Generation 3 vendors don't build a solution solely to solve current problems. They show the customer a path to the bigger outcome. And a by-product of achieving the bigger

24

outcome is solving the current problems. The focus is on achieving a new to-be state, not solving current problems. But they solve the problems.

Marc Benioff, CEO of Salesforce, has said:

> You must always be able to predict what's next and then have the flexibility to evolve.
> (Brainyquotes)

Both customers and vendors benefit from this mantra—from this focus on future outcomes. And both benefit from solving current customer problems as a by-product of enabling that future outcome.

Comparing the 3 Generations — The Story of the Three Entrepreneurs

Three entrepreneurs, each wanting to start a business, met with a hungry man.

'What do you want?' the first entrepreneur said.

'I want a sandwich.'

So, the first entrepreneur opened a sandwich store.

'What's your problem?' the second entrepreneur said.

'I don't have any food.'

The second entrepreneur opened a supermarket.

'What outcome do you want to achieve?' the third entrepreneur said.

The hungry man, who was overweight, looked puzzled.

'Do you want to be full and nourished?' the entrepreneur said.

The man agreed.

The third entrepreneur invented a pill. It contains all the necessary vitamins, minerals and proteins. When eaten, the pill creates foam in the stomach. The foam fools the body into thinking it's full.

The third entrepreneur just bought a mansion in the Bahamas.

The point of the story is true breakthroughs don't come from asking the customers what they want or about their current problems. Using these approaches would never have produced the printing press, the steam engine, radio, television, iPhones and iPads or 3D printing.

Outcome-driven thinking offers the best chance to develop unique ideas.

Generation 3 vendors expand their focus from product outcomes (the direct benefits from use of their products or services) to success outcomes (the broader outcome the customer wants to achieve).

Whenever someone buys a product or service, there is an outcome they want to achieve. In business there are two types of outcome—product outcomes and success outcomes.

Customers don't care about a vendor's product or service, they only care about the outcome they want to achieve—the success outcome.

What Outcome to Focus on?

Enabling customers to achieve an outcome is central to Generation 3 Customer Success. But people use the word outcome in so many ways that its meaning has become fuzzy. Let's start by clarifying the idea of an outcome in the context of Generation 3 Customer Success.

Whenever someone buys a product or service, they have an outcome to achieve. Think about anything people spend money on, and there'll be an outcome that it addresses. They buy a hamburger to be full; they buy a movie ticket to be entertained; they buy a sports car to be noticed (see Fig 10 on the following page).

Fig 10: Every purchase has an outcome

Two Types of Outcome — Product Outcomes and Success Outcomes

Product outcomes are the direct benefit of using a product or service.

In most cases, the customer has a bigger outcome they want to achieve. The product outcome is a means to an end, not an end in itself. We call the bigger outcome the customer wants to achieve the success outcome. It's what the customer considers success.

The relationship between product outcomes and success outcomes looks like this:

Fig 11: Relationship: Product and success outcomes

To illustrate. Imagine someone goes to a hardware store to buy a drill bit. The hardware store manager knows the person doesn't want to own a drill bit for its own sake. The person wants to drill a hole in the wall. The direct benefit of owning a drill bit is the hole in the wall. The hole is the product outcome.

But the customer doesn't want a hole in the wall for its own sake either. They want to hang a photo or picture—perhaps a family photo. The family photo hanging on the lounge room wall is the success outcome.

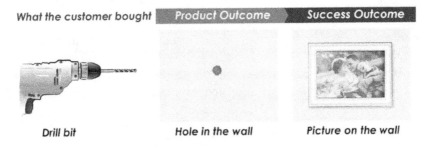

Fig 12: Success is the picture hanging on the wall

A restaurant provides another example. The restaurant offers good food and service. People will go to the restaurant to enjoy the food and service. Enjoyable food is the product outcome—the direct benefit of the restaurant's product and service.

But people don't go to the restaurant for the food alone. They go for an enjoyable evening with family or friends, or perhaps for a business meeting. The success outcome is a good evening out, or a successful business meal. Enjoyable food is part of the equation, but not enough by itself.

Fig 13: Success is a good night out

Characteristics of a Success Outcome

A success outcome has two elements. First, it creates a new to-be state. When people buy something, they have a to-be state they want to achieve. When they buy a movie ticket, the state they hope for is 'entertained'. When they buy a drill bit the to-be state is the family photo hanging on the wall; when they go to a restaurant the to-be state is social or business success.

Second, the success outcome has an emotional connection for the customer. The to-be state is something they want. The person hanging the family photo wants to feel the satisfaction of hanging the photo. The restaurant goers want the emotional connection with family or friends or the strong business connection.

A success outcome, when achieved, delivers both elements—a new to-be state and emotional satisfaction. Every organisation serves at least one success outcome.

Customers Don't Care About a Vendor's Products or Services

In technology, a product or service is a means to an end for the customer. They don't buy software because they want to own a software package. Or begin a major IT development to own a new set of code. Or contract for consulting services to own a report. They pay the money for the outcome these products or services can help them achieve.

They also don't care about the direct benefits from the vendor's product or service. This is a critical piece of thinking on success outcomes, so it's worth repeating. They don't care about the direct benefits from the vendor's product or service.

This statement is exaggerated for effect. Of course, the customers like the benefits. But only if they're also achieving the success outcome to which the vendor's products and services contribute.

Most Generation 2 vendors believe they must focus on and prove the direct benefits from their product or service. The better Generation 2 vendors measure these direct benefits. They promote the benefits their products or services produce—their product outcome. Generation 3 vendors understand the benefits from their products and service aren't an end in themselves. These benefits are also a means to an end. They contribute to achievement of a broader outcome, a broader to-be state the customer needs to achieve—the success outcome.

Generation 3 Vendors Focus on Success Outcomes

Generation 2 vendors, particularly non-subscription vendors, focus on their product outcome. The customer owns any elements outside the product outcome. If things go wrong with those other elements, it isn't the vendor's fault. If the project fails, the vendor can deny responsibility. The vendors don't like a failed project, but the financial impact on them isn't large.

For subscription-pricing vendors, things are different. If a project isn't successful, it doesn't matter who's at fault. They lose future business. Usage of their products or services won't go up and may even go down or be cancelled. Often through no fault of their own.

Generation 3 vendors have learned they can't ignore the things outside the immediate scope of their products and services. They need to do all they can to help the customer achieve the success outcome.

Jay Cao is Vice President, Greater China, of QAD, an ERP software company. A few years ago, one of their larger customers advised Jay they planned to replace QAD's software. The customer, a Taiwanese automotive components manufacturer operating in China, was unhappy with the effectiveness of their operations. They believed replacing the software would allow them to improve effectiveness and reduce costs.

The customer wasn't using QAD's software well. A Generation 2 vendor would have tried to retain the customer by showing how much better they could use the software and the benefits that would flow. In other words, improving the product outcome.

But Jay's team didn't do that. They focused on the success outcome the customer wanted—effective operations. And they had success consultants who knew how to improve operational effectiveness. So, they submitted a US$100,000 proposal to conduct a complete review of the customer's operations.

The customer accepted the proposal. The study took three months. Jay's team provided an incredible report that mapped out a clear path to operational effectiveness. The report delighted the customer who accepted the recommendations.

The customer then agreed to convert to the Cloud. They also signed contracts for substantial services. In total, over US$1,000,000 in contracts covering multiple years. An amazing turnaround driven by focusing on success outcomes not product outcomes.

Definition of a Success Outcome

A success outcome is an ongoing business result the top management of the customer would regard as success. Generation 3 vendors are the primary external enabler for the success outcome.

Let's break the definition down. First, a success outcome is an ongoing business result. The vendor helps the customer create a new to-be state. It's an ongoing to-be state, not a one-off event. It should be measurable, and the customer and vendor should jointly measure it over time. Even organisations not in business, such as government

32

departments, have results to achieve. And success outcomes should describe the ongoing improvement in the results they deliver.

Next, a success outcome is something top management of the customer would regard as a success. It can't be trivial. And it must be something the top management can understand and relate to. When they hear the success outcome, they should have an idea of the to-be state created. No technology jargon, no technical words.

Finally, the vendor must be the largest external provider of products and/or services for enablement of the success outcome. If the vendor isn't the largest external enabler, they've chosen the wrong success outcome to serve. Or they must have a plan to become the largest enabler.

Why Generation 3 Vendors Focus on Success Outcomes

Revenue

Growing recurring, loyal revenue is the primary focus. They do this by reducing churn, increasing upsell and cross-sell and improving new customer win-rates.

Reducing Risk

Let's go back to the drill bit. Imagine the customer doesn't hang the family portrait well. Perhaps they hang it in the wrong place and it doesn't look right. Or they hit electrical wiring in the wall and hurt themselves. The drill bit worked, but the customer got it wrong. They didn't achieve their success outcome.

That's not the fault of the hardware store manager. But here's the problem. The next time that customer has a job to do, they'll hire a handyman to do the job. They won't buy anything from the hardware store. The hardware store loses future revenue when the success outcome isn't achieved. Through no fault of their own.

The same thing can happen to the restaurant. The food and service were great for a family trying to enjoy a night out. But they didn't have fun. The kids kept playing on their phones and not engaging with the parents. Someone at the next table was loud and obnoxious. The family did not have a fun night out.

It's not the fault of the restaurant owner that the kids wouldn't engage, or that someone was loud. But the family won't go back to that restaurant. The restaurant will lose future revenue through no fault of its own.

Let's look at an example from the technology industry. Consider a marketing automation vendor. The customer contracts to use a marketing automation Cloud service. The customer will use the system to run email, social media and content marketing campaigns. The customer's marketing team delivers on the project plan for each campaign perfectly. The activity, response, efficiency and even value metrics are all where the vendor would expect them to be. The vendor has delivered the expected product outcome.

But the success outcome for this customer is reaching a pipeline value needed to deliver the sales targets. Let's say the pipeline does not eventuate. Through no fault of the marketing automation vendor. Perhaps the amount of resources dedicated to follow-up was insufficient. Or there was a breakdown in sales. Or the messages in the marketing campaigns did not resonate. It doesn't matter. The outcome the customer wanted to achieve was a pipeline of a certain value. The customer didn't achieve that outcome.

The customer might then decide that using a marketing automation service isn't the right approach for them. They think outsourcing the entire pipeline generation would work better. In that case, the marketing automation vendor will lose the customer and the recurring revenue, through no fault of its own.

If the customer doesn't achieve their success outcome, they'll consider the project a failure. Generation 3 vendors have realised helping with all aspects of the success outcome reduces risk of failure. And this increases the chance of future revenue growth.

Stickiness — The Safest Place to Be Is on a Winning Team

Let's use a sports analogy to make a related point.

Think of a sports team that goes through a slump. As the number of losing games grows, the clamour for change increases. The coach or manager will have to make changes to the team. They'll have to drop players, even if the players' form is okay. The coach or manager must act.

Now consider the reverse. Think about teams on a winning streak. Even if one or two team members aren't playing well, the coach or manager won't drop them. The coach or manager is likely to say, 'It's okay, they're just going through a temporary form slump, they'll bounce back.' The coach or manager knows that dropping players may change the dynamics and result in the team losing. They don't want to risk that.

The same principle applies to technology vendors. If the customer achieves their success outcome, they won't drop any vendors. And here's the interesting corollary. Even if the vendor's product outcome isn't great, the customer still won't drop them. Just like the sports coach or manager, they don't want to upset a winning streak.

Achievement of the success outcome has a far greater impact on future revenue than the product outcome. Generation 3 vendors have learned to make the success outcome their top priority.

Winning Deals

The customer has an outcome they want to achieve. They know they need technology products and services as part of achieving that outcome. They've done some research and chosen three vendors with which to talk.

The first vendor asks about the customer's problems and shows how well the product solves those problems. The solution looks good, and the vendor shows how to calculate ROI on the products. The customer must get the other elements needed for the success outcome together, but the product outcome looks good.

The second vendor alerts the customer to problems they weren't aware they had. It proves to be an eye-opener for the customer. The vendor shows how their product is uniquely suited to solving these new problems. And shows how they can solve the problems the customer already knew about. The customer likes the solution and its higher ROI. The customer still must get the other elements of the success outcome in place, but this product outcome looks even stronger.

The third vendor listens to the customer's problems and makes it clear they understand them. They then introduce a broader outcome the customer could achieve—the success outcome. Which would also solve the current problems. The success outcome would create a new to-be state. The customer can envisage that to-be state, and realise they want to achieve it. The vendor then shows they understand all aspects needed to achieve the success outcome. They have a good product, and they also know about the other elements the customer will need. They can help with most of those other elements, either through products or advice and guidance.

Customers care about the bigger outcome they want to achieve—the success outcome. The third vendor has focused on the thing the customer really cares about. And this creates a much stronger emotional bond, which increases the chance of winning. The third vendor looks different from and better than the competitors.

Getting Projects Approved

One of the biggest issues faced by vendors is the 'do nothing' decision. Generation 3 vendors have learned the best way to get a project approved is to show the value from achieving or improving a success outcome. The ROI on achieving a success outcome exceeds the ROI from a product outcome. As a result, a success outcome will garner greater interest at the top levels than a product outcome. And it's more likely to show a return the top executives will invest in.

Generation 3 vendors identify projects that enable or improve success outcomes. The business case focuses on the improvement in that success outcome. The product outcome is a footnote. These projects are more likely to be approved. Generation 3 vendors sell the value of a success outcome, not the value of a product outcome.

The Missing Link

Generation 2 vendors have long understood they can't sell based on features. They teach their salespeople to show the benefits. If they leave it up to the customer to make the link between features and benefits, the customer might not get it right. So, the salespeople articulate the benefits. And they sell benefits, not features.

The better Generation 2 vendors go past benefits and talk about value. They show the returns from their products and services. They often have Return on Investment models to quantify expected returns. The models look impressive.

But the customer doesn't care about the vendor's products and services. They care about the broader outcome they want to achieve—the success outcome. The Generation 2 vendors don't make the link between their product value (product outcome) and the success outcome. They leave it to the customer to make that link. Which may or may not happen.

Selling product outcomes without showing the link to the success outcome is the same as selling features without showing the link to the benefits.

Growth — 'There's Gold in Those Hills'

Clarity on the success outcome opens new growth opportunities for vendors. Generation 3 offers nine different methods for generating growth ideas based on the success outcome. We cover these in detail in Part 6 – Generation 3 Growth Planning.

What Vendors Can Do to Improve the Success Outcome

We've discussed why Generation 3 vendors focus on success outcomes. But what can they do to improve the achievement of the success outcome?

Let's go back to the drill bit example again. What can the hardware store manager do about the customer's success outcome of getting the family portrait hanging on the wall? The store could offer tip sheets or guides. They could place tip sheets on common jobs such as hanging a picture next to the drill bit display. Or they could have a website with links to YouTube videos on handyman tasks. Or they could offer in-store advice or courses.

What about the restaurant? Perhaps they're a family restaurant and the success outcome for customer is a fun family night out. Instead of battling to get kids off their phones, the restaurant could offer some apps that engage the whole family. Perhaps a trivia quiz. Families could compete between tables, with a big ice cream dessert for the winning kids.

Now let's look at our technology example, the marketing automation vendor. How could the vendor improve the outcome of 'pipeline achieved'? The vendor could provide guidance on marketing messaging or on the most successful marketing follow-up techniques or on how to develop a service level agreement between marketing and sales.

The vendor understands the success outcome and everything the customer needs to achieve it. They then do more to enable that success outcome.

ServiceNow (an IT Service Management company) focuses beyond the product outcome. David Oakley, Managing Director of Australia and New Zealand, said:

We have a program called Inspire. Under this, we agree a vision with the customer. We define what success looks like at various levels in the organisation. We do a business value analysis (partly before the sale and partly after the sale) to define what we'll both focus on and how we'll measure results. And we then build a success plan to get the customer there.

PART 2
DEEP ENGAGEMENT

Generation 3 uses DEEP Engagement.

DEEP Engagement has four phases—Develop, Evaluate, Execute, Prosper.

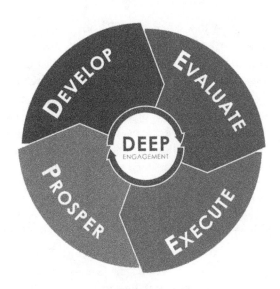

Fig 14: The four phases of DEEP Engagement

DEEP Engagement

DEEP Engagement has four phases—Develop, Evaluate, Execute and Prosper. Let's look at each.

Develop

In the Develop phase, Generation 3 vendors create interest in improving the success outcome they serve. Improving the success outcome requires projects. If the vendor has chosen their success outcome well, the projects will need products and/or services from the vendor.

Marketing leads the work in the Develop phase. And Sales delivers the same messages in their one-on-one engagement with customers.

41

The Develop phase is relevant for both existing customers and new customer lead generation.

Generation 3 marketers have learned not to focus on products. They focus on success outcomes. The logic is simple. Customers and prospects only care about their success outcome. If the marketing and sales messages focus on the success outcome, the customers and prospects will pay attention. If the marketing and sales messages focus on products and services, the customers and prospects will ignore them.

There's much to like in the work of CEB (now part of Gartner) and published in the second of their *Challenger Sale* series, *The Challenger Customer* (Adamson, 2015) The authors talk about the importance of consensus in decision-making on technology related projects. They discuss the difficulty of achieving consensus because of the diversity in organisations. Everyone has a different opinion and different needs. Achieving consensus requires tailoring for group consensus. The authors show that tailoring messages to each individual decreases consensus. It results in a minimalist set of requirements. Because that's all the group can agree on.

The authors also discuss Commercial Insight—providing information or insight that causes the customer to rethink aspects of their business.

The concepts of tailoring for consensus and Commercial Insight resonate for Generation 3 vendors. Generation 3 vendors use success outcomes as the consistent theme around which to drive this consensus and insight.

A success outcome has two characteristics. First, it describes a to-be state. For example, the family portrait is hung on the wall or the night out at a restaurant was enjoyed. Second, the success outcome has an emotional connection for the customer. It's something the customer wants.

In marketing messages, Generation 3 vendors emphasise the importance of the success outcome. For some vendors the success outcome is self-evident. Its importance needs no promotion. For example, a marketing automation vendor might serve a success outcome of 'pipeline generated'. They don't need to convince their customers of the importance of an adequate pipeline.

For other vendors, the success outcome may itself deliver insight. For example, a content management vendor will help organisations make good decisions. They may also offer workflow (processes for how specific decisions are made) and governance (who has access to sensitive information and what information should be considered when making decisions). Their success outcome might be 'informed and governed decisions'. Some customers may not have considered their need in these terms. But once they hear the phrase, it resonates. The customers realise they want informed and governed decisions. That's a to-be state that appeals to them. And they realise they need all three elements offered by this vendor.

Generation 3 vendors use the success outcome as a unifying theme—a way to build consensus. For example, government departments would align around achieving a to-be state (success outcome) of making informed and governed decisions.

Content Marketing

The vendor can use traditional content marketing to provide further insight. The *Challenger Sale* authors discuss how being a 'thought leader' isn't good enough anymore. Content marketing that simply confirms knowledge or opinions already held by the customer doesn't help. The content must offer new insight.

Generation 3 vendors provide insight based on the success outcome they serve. Articles, podcasts, webinars, blogs, etc. can cover the benefits of achieving the success outcome. Or the costs and risks of not achieving the success outcome. They can offer new methods for achieving or improving the success outcome. They can benchmark the success outcome. In all cases the content marketing reinforces the need to improve the success outcome.

Sales

The sales teams can promote the same ideas through their direct engagement with customers. And salespeople increase their access to senior executives by focusing on success outcomes. Executives don't want to discuss products. They want to discuss outcomes.

Summary

In the Develop phase, the vendor has two objectives. First, ensure the customer sees the importance of the vendor's success outcome. Second, ensure the customer sees the vendor as best able to help achieve or improve that success outcome.

MuleSoft provides integration software for connecting applications, data and devices. They use outcomes as part of their marketing message. Will Bosma, Vice President, Asia Pacific, said:

At a high level, we're becoming known for enabling 'application networks'. The outcome for customers is the easy connection of applications across any device. Think of it like connecting a new PC to a network. It should be that easy to connect applications. That's the to-be state we can create.

At a more detailed level, we've distilled what customers are looking for into six main outcomes. We've developed IP to help with all aspects of achieving each outcome. Our marketing promotes these outcomes. To illustrate, a common to-be state needed is 'legacy applications modernised'. This extends the life of the legacy applications while the business moves to SaaS applications. We can show customers how to achieve this outcome.

Evaluate

Generation 3 vendors of simpler products ensure the evaluation phase is as automated as possible. They use their own products and partner products to cover everything the customer needs to achieve the success outcome.

Generation 3 vendors of complex offerings identify projects to improve the success outcome. They do this with the customer—it's a joint activity. The customer evaluates the projects and decides which ones will proceed. The process is a recurring one—it happens every year or every quarter.

The work done by CEB in the *Challenger Sale* series (Dixon M. a., 2011), (Adamson, 2015) gives insight into the need for early engagement by the vendor. But CEB estimates the average buying process is 57% complete before the buyer talks to the vendor. The buyer has already decided the problems they'll solve and the requirements that will drive their purchase. And the lack of consensus within the buying organisation keeps the requirements to a bare minimum. These minimal requirements mean the customer doesn't place value on the extra things a vendor can do. And this in turn drives down what the buyer will pay. Vendors can end up in a race to the bottom on price.

In existing customers, Generation 3 vendors have learned how to become involved in the buying process at the very start. They use the Evaluate phase to help the customer identify projects that will improve the success outcome. They work jointly with the customer as they evaluate potential projects. And the vendors are paid for at least some of their work in this phase.

New Relic is a Digital Performance Monitoring and Management company. They engage jointly with their customers to identify potential projects. Greg Taylor, the Group Vice President, APAC, said:

When customers first start with us, they begin at the technical level. They track how well their application, website or mobile offering is performing.

Once that's working, we look for opportunities for improvement. With the customer's permission we can see what's happening in their operations. Our customer success team, using metrics and analysis, looks for opportunities for improvement. The customer and our team may go up to the application layer. For example, we helped an online clothing retailer develop and capture metrics to give instant feedback on their performance.

In other cases, we identify technical improvements. For example, getting more out of their infrastructure service from, say, AWS, Azure or Google.

Having helped them identify opportunities for improvement, we work with them to determine which projects will proceed. And then work to realise the improvements.

Execute

The next phase of DEEP Engagement focuses on delivering the outcome for approved projects. The purpose of this phase is to deliver and measure the improvements in the success outcome.

For vendors with complex offerings, Services leads the work in this phase. In many projects, the Success Consultants (more on this role later) involved in the Evaluate phase will also be involved in the Execute phase.

For vendors of simpler products, the onboarding process involves much more productisation. They have much less reliance on consulting and other services. We'll cover this more in Section 8, Bridging the Outcome Gap.

QAD, an ERP software company, sets objectives and measures results for qualifying projects. Anton Chilton, Chief, Global Field Operations, said:

> *We have three levels for setting project objectives and measuring results. Level 1 is a general objective such as improving customer satisfaction. Level 2 introduces a KPI, e.g. improve customer satisfaction by increasing Delivered In Full On Time (DIFOT) from 90% to 95%. Level 3 quantifies the benefit to the customer, e.g. increase profit by $10m by increasing DIFOT from 90% to 95%.*

Prosper

Project success delivers business returns for the customer. The project teams have achieved or improved the success outcome. But customers can't assume the improvement will continue. They must monitor and nurture the results. And the results can be further improved, particularly as business conditions evolve. A continuous improvement approach will help ensure the customer enjoys ongoing and increasing benefits from the success outcome.

The customer and vendor should work together to create a monitoring process. Cloud implementations give the vendor an opportunity to monitor in a much more meaningful way. The vendor has access to much more information from the customer's systems.

With the customer's permission, the vendor can analyse how the business functions. Early warning and alerts can trigger action earlier.

In Generation 3 vendors, the role of the Support department has evolved. In the past, the Support department reacted to product problems when notified by the customer. Now they're becoming proactive departments, reaching out before customers report problems. Many are developing predictive skills, identifying circumstances that could lead to problems. They also play a far more central role in monitoring success outcomes and ensuring reporting to the customer and vendor.

ServiceNow is an IT Service Management company. They see the benefit of continuously improving the outcomes achieved by their customers. David Oakley, Managing Director, ANZ, said:

We're sitting on a wealth of data. We have gathered information from customers opting into the program, and we can now benchmark them. We compare 23 KPIs on items such as how long it takes to resolve an issue, how long to fill a request and so on. The next step is for us to pro-actively reach out to customers that appear to be low on a benchmark and suggest ideas for how to improve that area of their operations. For example, we can look at their data and help them with routing. We can tell them if they'd routed a request with specific keywords to a particular group of resolvers, they'd be right 98% of the time. That process can then be automated. It saves requests sitting in a holding pattern waiting to be reviewed, which improves the service outcome delivered by IT.

Quick Wins

While Generation 3 vendors implement all DEEP steps, they don't need to finish to enjoy quick wins. The messaging around success outcomes can be used immediately in sales deals. Marketing can base a campaign around the success outcome. Services can start agreeing project objectives with customers. These quick wins help the vendor evolve to Generation 3.

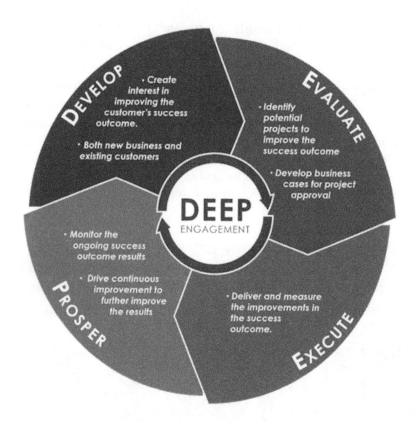

Fig 15: The focus at each stage of DEEP Engagement

> **DEEP Engagement provides a framework to develop an ideal customer lifecycle.**
>
> ---
>
> The lifecycle will differ depending on complexity of the products and services.
>
> Generation 3 vendors know not all customers will follow the ideal customer lifecycle. They have alternative methods for engaging with these other customers.

Ideal Customers

Generation 3 vendors have a model for engaging with their ideal customers. They strive to move customers to this ideal model. Ideal customers not only spend more money with the vendor, they're great references for new customer sales. But Generation 3 vendors understand not all customers will engage using the ideal model. So, they have alternative approaches available. In this book, we'll concentrate on the ideal customer lifecycle.

Customer Lifecycle

Generation 3 vendors have mapped out the major steps in their engagement with customers. The steps cover activities in marketing, sales, services and support—the whole lifecycle of direct engagement with the customer. Vendors of complex offerings have agreed the lifecycle with the customer. Most steps involve joint activity between the vendor and customer. They have also agreed the deliverables from each step and their respective responsibilities.

Vendors of simpler products have different customer lifecycles. But they still understand, monitor and drive that lifecycle.

Vendors of Complex Offerings

Generation 3 vendors with complex offerings use the following techniques to improve results.

Periodic Business Reviews

Generation 3 vendors conduct regular business reviews with customer executives. The vendor and customer jointly focus on the success outcome. They discuss results achieved, changes in strategies and other factors affecting the success outcome, and next steps in improving the success outcome. They don't discuss the vendor's products or services.

Success Consulting

Generation 3 vendors offer consulting on the success outcome, not just the product outcome. The larger the gap between the product outcome and success outcome, the more Success Consultants can help. Success Consultants understand all elements required for the customer to achieve the success outcome. The Success Consultants are typically senior and expensive people. They work with the customer to develop a plan to enable or improve the success outcome. Because they focus on the success outcome and not the product outcome, customers are willing to pay for their time. Their rates are much higher than any other of the vendor's consultants.

We'll cover this in more detail in Section 5 — Success Consulting.

The 10% Sale — Business Case Studies

During periodic business reviews, the customer or vendor identify opportunities for improvement in the success outcome. These improvement opportunities would each result in a project. If a project went ahead, the customer would need the vendor's products and services. But Generation 3 vendors don't try to sell products or services right away. Instead, they propose a joint study to determine whether a business case for a project exists. The joint report provides all the information an executive committee or board of directors need to decide on a project.

Success consultants lead business case studies. As a rule of thumb, the price for the study is about 10% of the cost for the overall project. To illustrate, if the overall project would require a $100,000 investment, the business case study has a $10,000 price.

The business case study provides customer executives with a detailed insight into the project, before having to commit. This reduces risk for the executives and increases the chance of them approving the project. And if the project does go ahead, the total cost is about the same. The business case study covers activities normally performed early in a project anyway. To continue the example above, if the project cost estimate is $100,000 and the vendor conducts a $10,000 study, the remaining project costs will be a little over $90,000.

A business case study takes risk out of project decisions for the customer. It's also a great way for vendors to qualify. If the customer won't pay 10% for a study, they aren't interested in the project. It's much better for the vendor to find this out early. The sales team can re-sell the value of the project or they can walk away. Either way, they don't waste resources developing free proposals the customers won't approve.

MuleSoft provides integration software for connecting applications, data and devices. They employ this approach. Brent Grimes, Vice President, Global Customer Success, said:

> We develop a Case for Action using a management consulting approach. We work with the customer to determine if a case for action on a project exists. There's a price for this service. But we sometimes reduce that price where the customer deeply engages in the assessment, particularly at the executive level. We also offer a maturity study, where we analyse the six pillars of the customer's integration capability and provide a detailed report.

Comprehensive, Joint Measurement

The vendor monitors entry-level measures such as churn and product usage internally. They also track the effectiveness of the customer lifecycle. Together with the customer, they monitor product outcomes, success outcomes and project outcomes. We'll cover this in more detail in Section 7 — Customer Success Measurement.

Realistic Expectations

Vendors understand the need for a customer success program. The program will not only help protect and grow their own recurring revenue, it will improve the success of the customer.

If the vendors expect universal acclaim from customers, they're in for a disappointment. Lots of customers will feel they've heard it all before. Vendors often lay claim to being customer-centric. They promise wonderful returns from the customer's investment. The customers often feel disappointed.

The announcement by a vendor of their brand-new customer success program will result in cautious interest. After explaining the program, some customers will join with enthusiasm. Others may show willingness to experiment. Still others will remain unconvinced and want things to continue unchanged.

Generation 3 vendors start with the enthusiastic customers. They pilot the program with willing participants before attempting a broader rollout. We'll cover this in more detail in Part 5 — Implementing Generation 3 Customer Success.

In the meantime, Generation 3 vendors apply customer success approaches to their other customers. At a minimum, they track entry-level measures such as churn and product usage. Where possible, they monitor product outcomes. For some, they may also monitor success outcomes.

Over time, Generation 3 vendors move more customers into the DEEP Engagement program. But each vendor will need a method for engaging with those customers that don't take part. That's okay. A Generation 3 vendor doesn't need all customers to be in the DEEP program.

Generation 3 Customer Success will improve new business win rates. To do that, the vendor needs Generation 3 references. In the early stages of a DEEP implementation, there's a focus on developing these references. The references help the vendor win new business and convert other customers to DEEP Engagement.

Generation 3 vendors with complex offerings use a recurring lifecycle to engage with key customers.

The lifecycle will be different for each vendor.

Each step focuses on the success outcome, and each has a clear deliverable.

Lifecycle for Vendors with Complex Offerings

This section provides an example of a lifecycle for vendors with more complex offerings. Vendors with simpler offerings are much more attuned to productising their lifecycle. Vendors of complex products find it more difficult to productise, so rely more on consulting and services.

Phase 1 – Develop

The aim is to create interest in improving the success outcome. Campaigns drive this interest.

Marketing leads the work in the Develop phase. And Sales delivers the same messages in their one-on-one engagement with customers. The Develop phase is relevant for both existing customers and new customer lead generation.

While the steps vary by vendor, there's a common call-to-action for customers—improve your success outcome. The marketing messages then position the vendor as best able to help.

Phase 2 – Evaluate

Generation 3 vendors don't try to sell products in the early steps of this phase. With the customer, they jointly evaluate potential projects to improve the success outcome. They know if the right projects proceed, the customer will buy more products and services from them. For Generation 3 vendors with more complex products, the following steps are typical:

The Periodic Business Review involves customer executives and the sales and success consulting team. For some customers, vendor executives may also attend. Both the vendor and customer prepare before engaging with the customer executives.

Preparation would typically involve the following:

- identification of any trends or changes in the industry, market, regulations, etc. affecting the success outcome
- success outcome KPIs with a focus on any gaps between actual and target
- benchmarks against external data, where available
- identification of potential improvement areas

The customer and vendor collaborate on preparation for the review meeting. The customer executives should see the reports and information as coming from both the vendor and their own staff. This lends credibility and reinforces the vendor's focus on the customer's success outcome.

Deliverable – a briefing suitable for the customer executives.

Periodic Business Review

Periodic Business Reviews work best if the key customer executives are together. But sometimes this isn't practical, and the vendor needs to work with executives one-on-one.

The agenda of a Periodic Business Review will typically have the following items:

- update by the customer executives on strategies, initiatives and focus
- update by the vendor on any strategic or organisation changes affecting the vendor's ability to enable the success outcome—this should <u>not</u> include updates on products or services
- identification of any trends or changes in the industry, market, regulations, etc. affecting the success outcome
- review of success outcome KPIs with a focus on any gaps between actual and target
- benchmarks against external data, where available

- identification of potential improvement areas
- selection of potential improvement areas for further analysis
- identification of the customer's executive sponsor for each of the selected areas

Deliverable – a short list of potential improvement areas requiring further analysis.

High Level Business Case Analysis

The customer and vendor jointly analyse each potential improvement area. For each, they'll agree:

- the potential to-be state
- the major steps required to achieve that new to-be state
- a high-level business case—the size of the prize

Deliverable – a joint report providing the high-level business analysis for each potential improvement area. The business case (size of the prize) will be signed off by each relevant executive sponsor. It does not include any references to the vendor's products or services. It's a business analysis framed by the success outcome.

Potential Projects Review

The attendees at the periodic business review meet again to review the high-level business cases. Typically, the vendor Success Consultant would lead the presentation. But everyone present should understand it's a joint presentation.

The customer executives decide on each potential improvement area. Possible decisions include:

- proceed to the next stage—for areas that look promising, the customer will ask the vendor to prepare a proposal for a business case study which will be a paid engagement for the vendor
- do nothing—areas that don't look promising will not proceed any further
- defer—some areas will be of interest, but the timing won't be right and the customer will hold these for future consideration

- further investigation—the executives did not feel they had enough information to decide the next step and the meeting will agree an action plan for further investigation

For any potential projects, there's a final test. The executives should confirm that funding for a project would be available if a positive business case exists. No-one wants to waste time if there's no chance of a project moving forward.

Deliverable – a list of potential projects proceeding to the next stage or requiring further investigation.

Detailed Business Case Analysis

To approve a sizeable project, most customers need a business case. Different companies have different business case formats. Before commencing, the joint team establishes the approval format required for each potential project. The customer's Chief Financial Officer usually provides this input. The final report should include all content required for approval in the format needed.

The finished report will typically include:

- the to-be state the project will deliver
- the major changes required to achieve the to-be state
- high-level solution designs
- a project plan setting out expected timelines and milestones
- detailed costing
- return on investment analysis—based on the return from improving the success outcome

The report isn't about implementing the vendor's products or services. It's a report about achieving or improving the success outcome. Improvements, particularly quick wins, may not be technology related. For example, the report might identify a gap in user knowledge that training could address.

It's possible the report may not identify a need for the vendor's products or services. The benefits may come from other areas such as training, process re-design or different engagement with partners. Generation 3 vendors accept not all projects will result in revenue for them. But they can still benefit—their credibility with the customer executives increases. The executives can see the vendor is focused on the success outcome, not just their own revenue. And the vendor's

Success Consultants have been paid for preparing the detailed business case anyway.

Before the final report, the sponsoring executive and the CFO receive a draft of the business case report. These executives verify any numbers, particularly the return on investment analysis, before the report is finalised.

The deliverable from this step is a detailed business case for each potential project. Each report should have all content required for project approval.

Project Decisions

The customer then takes each business case report through their internal approval process. Some projects may receive approval immediately, some may go to a budgeting process and others may not obtain approval.

Deliverable – a decision on each business case.

Phase 3 — Execute

The purpose of this phase is to deliver and measure the improvements in the success outcome. Services leads the work in this phase. In many projects, the Success Consultants involved in the Evaluate phase will continue in the Execute phase.

Here are some typical steps:

Project Set-up

The customer and vendor establish their project teams, executive sponsors and governance processes. They agree the business objective for the project. If they prepared a detailed business case in the Evaluate phase, they will already have the objective. The project objective should have a clear link to the success outcome.

Generation 3 vendors set real and measurable objectives for qualifying projects. Qualifying projects are those large enough to warrant a formal project structure, as opposed to small, quick projects. Ideally the objectives will be in the form of fiscal return on investment. A fall-back is to agree improvements in success measures or KPIs. All parties acknowledge the project objectives as joint objectives for the customer and vendor. They aren't a commitment from the vendor alone to deliver this result.

Most projects need a business solution design. Where a detailed business case exists, most of this design work will already have occurred. This reduces the time and cost in the project, which offsets the cost of the earlier business case preparation.

The final step is to hold a kick-off meeting. The team announces the project objectives, timeline and participants to the company. In better-run projects, the presentation includes a change management plan.

The deliverable from this step is a project plan and clearly defined mutual objectives.

Project Execution

Project execution uses a formal methodology agreed by all parties. It's typically the vendor's methodology. The methodology helps ensure focus on achievement of the project objectives. Every project meeting and steering committee meeting includes a review of progress towards the objectives. It's understood by everyone that go-live is a major milestone, but not the end of the project.

Deliverable – achievement of the project objectives.

Measure and Report

The project won't finish until the teams have measured results and reported back to the customer executives. At the beginning of the project, the project team established how and when to measure results. Depending on the project, the team gathered benchmark data.

After go-live, the combined project team confirms how and when to measure results. They capture benchmark data.

Once they've measured results, a presentation to the customer executives takes place. This happens regardless of whether the objectives were realised. If the teams achieved the objectives, then the executives offer plaudits to them both. If they didn't achieve the objectives, then the customer and vendor project teams jointly present lessons learnt. They don't try to lay blame. It's a joint report from the combined project teams to the executives. If the objectives weren't achieved, it's highly likely both sides could have done better. Both sides should be willing to acknowledge areas for improvement.

The combined teams should offer suggestions for rectification. The executives can then decide whether to take further action.

Deliverable — a report on the success or otherwise of the project.

Phase 4 — Prosper

In this phase, the customer and vendor monitor the success outcome KPIs over time. And they drive further improvements through continuous improvement.

Both parties establish ongoing analysis of the success outcome KPIs. And they agree on how to report these to the customer executives. They drive continuous improvement by going back to the Evaluate phase.

The Support department can play an important role in this phase. They can get much of the data needed. Modern Support departments no longer see themselves as reactive. They don't wait for the customer to advise of a problem. They've moved to a more pro-active approach. They identify potential problems before they occur, or as they occur, and act immediately.

Generation 3 Support departments go a step further. They play a role in gathering and analysing success outcome data, and in producing the necessary reports.

A series of principles guide the way Generation 3 vendors work.

Most vendors are already on the path to Generation 3. The Generation 3 Customer Success program helps them unify around a single theme—serving the success outcome.

Understanding All Elements of the Success Outcome

Generation 3 vendors understand their customers care about the success outcome, not the product outcome. So, they've learned how to help the customer with more of the success outcome. They don't ignore the product outcome. They know it's important to the relationship. But they also understand the product outcome is a means to an end, not an end in itself.

When they engage with customer executives, Generation 3 vendors talk about the success outcome. They show their knowledge of, and provide insight on, the success outcome. Over time they'll strive to do more and more of what the customer needs to achieve their success outcome.

Joint Engagement with Customers

Enabling a success outcome is usually complex, and each customer will have unique challenges. Generation 3 vendors have learned they can improve outcomes by pooling the skills and knowledge of the customer's team and their own team. At each stage of the customer lifecycle, they emphasise joint activity.

Generation 3 vendors ensure projects have measurable objectives that link to a success outcome. These objectives aren't commitments by the vendor to deliver that result. They're a joint commitment by the customer and vendor project teams to deliver that real and measurable outcome.

Segmentation by Engagement Model

Generation 3 vendors develop a customer lifecycle for their ideal customer. But they understand that not all customers want to work with them that way. So, they have engagement models that allow for alternative engagement approaches.

They've also learned they can use the customer's desired engagement approach as another criterion to segment their customers.

Measurement

Generation 3 vendors understand the need to monitor and measure the results they and their customers achieve. They work at four levels:

- entry-level measures—items such as churn, percentage of contracted users who are active and usage of key product features
- product outcomes—the direct benefits from using the vendor's products and services
- success outcomes—the measurable benefits from enabling the bigger outcome the customer wants to achieve
- project outcomes—measurable objectives that link to the success outcome the project serves

Generation 3 vendors also track the effectiveness of each step in the customer lifecycle.

We'll cover this in more detail in Section 7 — Customer Success Measurement.

Vendor Success Program vs Customer Success Program

Generation 3 vendors know they can't focus only on churn and product usage. If they do, they have a vendor success program, not a customer success program. They still track these entry-level measures—they still want to maximise short-term revenue. And they know they must deliver product outcomes. But they understand product outcomes aren't enough. They need to deliver success outcomes to secure their medium to long-term success.

Genuinely Helping with the Success Outcome

Customers know if a vendor doesn't understand the success outcome. Generation 3 vendors have learned they can damage their relationship if they try to bluff their way through.

Improving the Customer's Success Outcome Is an Ongoing Task

It's unlikely a success outcome will be fully achieved from an initial project. Even when the customer reaches the initial objectives, they'll want further improvement. In the event a customer says they're satisfied with the standard reached, the vendor can expand or change the success outcome they serve. We'll cover this in more depth in Part 6 — Generation 3 Growth Planning.

The Path to Enabling or Improving a Success Outcome Can Change

Lots of things can affect success outcomes, including changes in business environment, regulations, company strategies, competitors' strategies, technology and market trends. The customer may want to change the path to achieving the success outcome or may even want to vary the success outcome itself. Generation 3 vendors see this as both a challenge and an opportunity.

Focus on Deliverables (Outcomes) More Than Process

Generation 3 vendors have a customer lifecycle with defined steps. Each step has a deliverable or outcome. In most cases, the vendor and customer work together on the deliverable or outcome.

Generation 3 vendors have smart, competent people working for them. They've learned to focus their staff on the deliverables, rather than forcing staff to follow an inflexible process. Generation 3 vendors have processes but allow flexibility. They monitor outcomes, not compliance with process. But they do insist on minimum standards in quality of communication, proposals, reports, etc.

The staff of Generation 3 vendors understand they must meet the minimum standards. The staff are clear about the deliverables from each step of the customer lifecycle. And they're given the opportunity to adapt and improve how they achieve the deliverable or outcome at each step.

Generation 3 vendors have learned this approach improves staff motivation and retention. More importantly, it improves the quality of results achieved.

Focus on the Big Stuff

Generation 3 vendors and customer executives engage in joint planning. Generation 3 vendors ensure the focus stays on topics that could deliver big returns for the customer. They don't want to waste executives' time. If executives find themselves discussing topics that have little impact on business results, they'll soon stop attending. And if the topics can produce big results for the customer, they can produce more revenue for the vendor.

Sometimes executives introduce topics which don't advance the joint planning. Generation 3 vendors deal with these carefully. An executive may want to discuss the problem with the vendor in the meeting. This disrupts the agenda and may not interest other executives. The Generation 3 vendor will provide a quick update. They'll then suggest that a follow-up discussion with relevant support staff take place outside of the planning meeting.

Similarly, small topics sometimes arise. For example, someone may observe the need to train a small number of users. Generation 3 vendors try not to discuss that in the planning meeting. Again, they try to make it a separate discussion.

Generation 3 vendors stay focused on topics that can deliver big improvements in the success outcome.

Generation 3 Vendors Sell Projects Not Products

Vendors love their products. In front of executives, Generation 1 and even Generation 2 vendors can't resist telling the executives about their products. They forget that customers, particularly executives, don't care about the products.

Generation 3 vendors keep the conversation on the success outcome. With executives, they find it's rarely necessary to discuss product. They may need to describe the business changes needed to improve the success outcome. They don't need to describe how the software or services work.

Generation 3 vendors understand their customers don't get internal approval to buy products and services. They get approval to proceed with a project. The internal proposal doesn't only seek funding for the vendor's products, it includes all costs needed for the project. It's in the vendor's interest to ensure the customer has everything needed to have the project approved.

They've also learned the joint planning process should focus on potential projects. At every stage of the joint planning process, the focus remains on potential projects to enable or improve the success outcome.

Naming a Project

Generation 3 vendors have learned to suggest project names that relate to the success outcome or the objectives of each project. They know this helps keep everyone focused on the business outcome. And because success outcomes have an emotional connection for the customer, the customer tends to be more committed. They've learned not to name the project after their own products or services. For example, Generation 3 ERP vendors don't allow a project to become known as the ERP project.

New Visibility for the Vendor

Generation 2 customer engagement is typically transaction based. Either the customer has identified a problem and needs a solution, or the vendor has a new product to promote. Both parties focus on the immediate opportunity. They typically only talk about one potential project.

Generation 3 vendors have learned DEEP Engagement produces a wonderful by-product—two to three years' visibility into potential projects. The Evaluate phase identifies areas in which the executives have interest. Some of these areas will proceed to the Business Case step while others will remain on hold for future consideration. Either way, the vendor has insight into the areas the executives feel need attention. It's hard to imagine a better insight into projects the vendor may need to address over the next two to three years.

For the vendor, it provides an opportunity to fill any gaps in the product line. It provides insight into new skills, processes or systems they may need. And it provides an opportunity for them to decide how to bridge any gaps.

Eventually, the joint planning process produces a two- to three-year outlook updated every year.

MuleSoft provides integration software for connecting applications, data and devices and employs a multi-year approach. Will Bosma, Vice President, Asia Pacific, said:

> When we look at projects, we discuss possible future projects with the customer. With this insight, we can design the first project to make later projects easier. For example, we helped a health supplements company provide better insights for their outlets.
>
> But we also discussed two follow-on projects. The first was to use blockchain to establish a supply chain into China that could be authenticated. The Chinese customers wanted certainty the product they were buying was genuine. Blockchain provided this certainty. The second was an RFID project ensuring bottles weren't 're-used' by local manufacturers to sell fake products.
>
> By discussing future requirements when designing the first project, we made the later projects easier. And we gained strong insight into the future projects, which aided our forecasting and planning.

A New Relationship between IT Departments and Technology Vendors

IT departments are under more pressure to enable business results than ever before. Technology vendors, because of subscription pricing, have a greater need to enable customer success than ever before. The mutual interests are aligned as never before.

Generation 3 vendors bring new skills to the customer. They focus on exactly what the executives in the company want—outcomes. IT departments can use the greater skills of Generation 3 vendors, particularly the Success Consultants. They don't have to rely on in-house skills or outside consultants. They can work with the Generation 3 vendor for each success outcome.

The IT department can open doors for the Generation 3 vendor that might otherwise be closed. They can also provide the vendor with information on what's happening inside the customer organisation.

There's been a tendency at times for IT departments and technology vendors to be at loggerheads. Some vendors actively bypass the IT department. Generation 3 gives an opportunity for both parties to come back together in mutual support of customer success.

Most Vendors Are Already on the Path to Generation 3

Most vendors have already evolved aspects of their business beyond Generation 2. Adopting Generation 3 allows all parts of the business to align around one simple theme—enabling the success outcome.

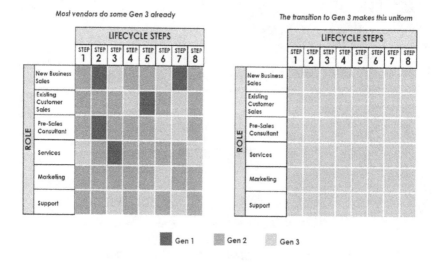

Fig 16: Gen 3 aligns business around success outcomes

Generation 3 Success Consultants help the customer with all aspects of achieving the success outcome.

And much of their work should be billable, even in 'pre-sales'.

Success Consulting is more valuable where the gap between the product outcome and the success outcome is larger.

A Different Type of Consultant

Generation 3 vendors with complex offerings use a different type of consultant for both sales and services. The Success Consultant understands everything required by the customer to achieve the success outcome.

They're different from Generation 2 pre-sales or business consultants. To illustrate, pre-sales consultants in ERP Software have a deep understanding of the software and can show how the software delivers direct benefits (product outcomes). They typically have great industry knowledge and understand the problems and challenges the industry faces. They can articulate how the software addresses the problems and challenges. They're smart, competent and have good customer presence. The customers like good Generation 2 pre-sales consultants. However, because the Generation 2 consultants focused on the vendor's products, the customer did not expect to pay for pre-sales activity.

Generation 3 Success Consultants in ERP understand what's required to achieve the customer's desired to-be state. They have an appreciation not only of the software, but of the processes, people skills and partners that play a role. When they write a business case, it's a business case for a project not for the software.

Success Consultants address a broad range of issues. They don't limit their focus to a set of problems the software can address. They identify everything the customer needs to achieve the success outcome. For many customers, this proves a godsend. Many customers struggle to understand everything they need to do to achieve their success outcome. It's often the first time they've tried. They need guidance and help.

It doesn't mean the Success Consultant can deliver every aspect. They may need the help of specialist consultants. But the Success Consultant provides the overall view. They provide the roadmap for achieving the success outcome. If customer executives seek and heed the advice of a Success Consultant, the vendor knows they have the right person for the job.

Success Consultants focus on success outcomes not products or services. They're no longer seen as pre-sales consultants selling products and services. So, customers will pay for their advice and guidance. This changes the pre-sales stage—the vendor doesn't carry all the risk and expense. The customer now pays for some pre-sales work. And the day rates for a Success Consultant should be high, to match their skill level and salary packages. But even at high day rates, good Success Consultants always have too much work. The customers love them.

It's often cheaper for the customer to use Success Consultants. To hire someone full-time with the skill of a Success Consultant would not make sense for most customers. The customer doesn't need their high-level skills all year but would have to pay the high salary. The alternative is to struggle along without those skills or to hire an outside consultant. And an outside consultant will often take time to get up to speed, and cost more overall than a vendor's Success Consultant.

The Success Consultant spends most of their time in the Evaluate phase of DEEP Engagement. But they also play a role in the Execute phase. Their role is to ensure the to-be state agreed by the customer as part of the Detailed Business Case Analysis is on-track. They play a Quality role, helping keep the project headed towards delivering the project objectives. And this work is also billable work.

Bridging the Outcome Gap

There's usually a gap between the product outcome and the success outcome. The vendor's products don't do everything the customer needs to achieve their success outcome. The larger this gap, the more opportunity for a Success Consultant to make an impact. Where the gap is large, the customer must bridge the gap themselves. Success

Consultants know how to bridge the gap and can help the customer do so.

Stefan de Haar led the South Asia region for QAD, an ERP software company. (He now leads the entire Asia-Pacific region.) QAD has an established lifecycle for ideal customers.

Stefan's team conducted a periodic business review with an automotive components customer. They identified potential improvements in the customer's operations. The customer engaged QAD to conduct a business case study. They wanted to know if a business case for making change existed. The study focused on the customer's Design, Plan and Make processes.

The report, written jointly by Prapan Potiratsombat (a Success Consultant) and the customer's staff:

- recommended a new to-be state—a new way of running these key operations

- gave a clear path for reaching the new to-be state

- re-aligned the customer's Key Performance Indicators for key processes

- quantified the business benefits of the changes in the operations and provided an ROI analysis

The report focused on the success outcome of operational effectiveness. It didn't need to mention software or product outcomes. It included everything required by the customer to get internal approval for the improvement project—which they got.

The customer then signed substantial services and software contracts with QAD covering multiple years. Stefan's team had again shown that focusing on the customer's success outcome results in large contracts and loyal customers.

Gen 3 vendors understand customer success is not a single department.

It affects all customer-facing parts of the business.

Two by-products of a successful Gen 3 Customer Success program are serving a higher purpose and a positive change in culture.

All customer-facing departments play a role in customer success. Sales will sell the vendor's ability to enable or improve the success outcome. Services projects will have measurable objectives that enable or improve the success outcome. Marketing will develop insights on how customers can enable or improve the success outcome.

Support will play a role in monitoring and measuring outcomes. Initially this may be product usage, but in time it can expand to measurement of product outcomes and success outcomes. Even R&D can use the lens of success outcomes to generate ideas for new products and services.

Steve Lucas, CEO of Marketo (Planhat, 2017), says:

> In Marketo, we have a Customer Success team and I will tell you what keeps me awake at night. I'm worrying about making sure that customer success is not just looked at as a group within an organisation. Customer success is a mandate of everyone. Number 1! So, that's the developer, the salesperson, that's whoever is taking support calls and yes, of course, the customer success manager. I view our customer success organisation as kind of a linchpin, so to speak, where they operate and orchestrate the notion of customer success across the entire organisation.

> If you look at Marketo, one of the things that I've done for our organisation is mandate the customer success metrics in everyone's compensation plan. So, it's not something that one person thinks about.

Generation 3 Customer Success affects everyone who engages with the customer. But each vendor will develop different approaches. The following section provides insights and thoughts to help develop each vendor's program.

Sales

Purpose

The purpose of the sales department is to secure and grow commercial relationships with customers. Salespeople with New Business responsibility win the initial relationship. Depending on the structure of the team, other people will then grow that relationship.

Roles

In New Business, salespeople link the customer's buying process with the vendor's selling process. Their initial task is to 'sell the dream'—to sell the importance of the success outcome (more on this in Part 3). They then help the prospect understand why the vendor can best enable that success outcome.

For existing customers, the salespeople's role is to:

- convert as many customers as possible to the vendor's ideal engagement model
- for ideal customers, manage the recurring customer lifecycle
- for non-ideal customers, identify potential projects in an ad-hoc fashion
- negotiate commercial terms
- manage relationships

The success consultant's role is to:

- identify potential projects to enable or improve the customer's success outcome
- work with the customer to analyse and create business cases for projects
- be a bridge between sales and services—develop the to-be state as part of a business case and then help enable the to-be state and project objectives
- deliver high margin services revenue

The 'pre-sales' consultant's role is:

- to prove the product can deliver the product element of the success outcome

Marketing

Purpose

- create desire for the success outcome the vendor serves
- associate the vendor with enablement of this success outcome
- identify and track triggers that would focus prospects on the vendor's success outcome

Services

Purpose

- generate references for enabling the success outcome
- deliver services at the right margin

Changes in Services

- focus project management on delivering project objectives, not just on going live
- ensure managed services also focus on success outcomes, not just a Service Level Agreement

Support

Purpose

- reactive
  - solve product problems reported by the customer
- proactive
  - identify problems or potential problems and help the customer solve them before they cause an issue
  - measure and report on all customer success KPIs, including success outcomes

R&D

Purpose

Deliver as much of the success outcome as possible through the product.

Changes in R&D

- link the product roadmap to the success outcome
- prioritise based on the level of contribution to the success outcome

Purpose and Culture

Most organisations understand that staff want to serve a higher purpose. Serving a higher purpose increases discretionary effort, reduces staff turnover and improves morale. Serving a higher purpose also affects culture in a positive way.

Angela Duckworth, in her best-selling book *Grit* (Duckworth, 2017), offers the following:

> *At its core, a culture is defined by the shared norms and values of a group of people. In other words, a distinct culture exists anytime a group of people are in consensus about how we do things around here and why.*

Generation 3 vendors have learned that focusing on the customer's success outcome provides a higher purpose. Everyone can see they're doing more than just selling and implementing products. They're making a measurable difference to the lives of their customers.

And by aligning all customer-facing departments around success outcomes, the culture changes. The old culture of 'customer first' was hard to translate into action. The culture of enabling the success outcome is clearer. And by focusing on deliverables at each step in the lifecycle, staff can make a difference in how they enable the success outcome.

Generation 3 vendors didn't start out to provide purpose and to change culture—but they're excellent by-products.

Section 7 — Customer Success Measurement

> **Generation 3 vendors monitor a comprehensive range of KPIs and metrics.**
>
> ---
>
> The entry-level measures, more focused on their own revenue, they do by themselves. The rest of the measures, they track with their customers.
>
> Generation 3 vendors measure at four levels—Entry-level, Product Outcome, Success Outcome, Project Outcome.
>
> They also track the effectiveness of each step of their ideal customer lifecycle.

Entry-level Measures

The following are examples of metrics focused on usage and renewals. Vendors track them for all customers. They have alerts to prompt action whenever the metrics lie outside defined ranges. Because these measures focus more on vendor success than customer success, the vendor needs to do them alone. As well as identifying at-risk contracts or customers, they can also identify opportunities for upsell and cross-sell.

Recurring Revenue

- ARR—Annual Recurring Revenue—the annualised value of current contracts
  or
- MRR—Monthly Recurring Revenue—the same but on a monthly basis

Lifetime Value (LTV)

- Total Revenue (or in some cases margin) derived from a customer—often expressed as an average across customers, so other analysis needs to account for outliers

- Customer Churn—the percentage of customers that leave in a period
- Gross Revenue Churn—the total value of contracts cancelled in a period
- Net Revenue Churn for Existing Customers—total value of contracts cancelled since the start of the period, netted against the increase in value of the contracts—through cross-sell and upsell—that were in place at the start of the period
- Net Revenue Churn in Total—as above plus the effect of new contracts (net new business or new logo business) begun after the start of the period

Usage

- Active Users—the percentage of subscription users who are active (a low percentage indicates high risk of subscriptions being cancelled)
- Feature/Function Usage—the percentage of advanced features in use (a low percentage indicates a need for training or consulting to improve customer return and reduce risk of churn)

Product Outcome Measures

These are the measurable benefits derived from a vendor's products and services. They vary depending on the products and services and the industry. To illustrate with marketing automation, measures might include:

- activity results such as percentage of emails opened or responded to
- value of leads generated

These measures focus on marketing-led activities and results. They're Generation 2 measures. They focus on the direct benefit from the use of the vendor's products and services. As with entry-level measures, Generation 3 vendors also track these. But Generation 3 vendors go a step further.

Success Outcome Measures

The customer cares most about the success outcome to which a vendor's products and services contribute. Generation 3 vendors know they can deliver the product outcome, but the customer can fail to achieve their success outcome. Even if it's not the vendor's fault, the vendor may still suffer. They've also learned there's a big upside in helping the customer achieve the success outcome. So, Generation 3 vendors track the success outcome as well.

Let's continue the example of marketing automation. The customer has a sales target to reach. They need a strong pipeline to reach the target. A percentage of that pipeline should come from marketing-generated leads. For the marketing automation vendor, the success outcome is the value of marketing-generated sales; that is, deals that close from leads generated by marketing. Let's emphasise that point. The success outcome is not the value of marketing-generated leads—that's a product outcome. The success outcome is the value of deals closed from marketing leads.

And that requires sales. But what if sales don't follow up the leads, so no deals are closed? Perhaps sales experienced poor quality leads in the past, so decided it isn't worth their while to follow up. There's a disconnect. Even if Marketing has changed and now produces great leads, the success outcome won't be achieved.

Senior customer executives will then need to act, and they might decide they need a different approach to lead generation. Or they bring in an outside consultant who recommends changes in marketing automation software. The existing marketing automation vendor could lose their customer, through no fault of their own.

A Generation 3 vendor wouldn't let that happen. They'd have a success consultant who understands the whole lifecycle from lead generation to deal closure. The success consultant would work with both sales and marketing to establish a service level agreement (SLA). Marketing would drive the lead further down the sales cycle to the point where the sales team needs to step in. And sales would then step in in a timely fashion. Both parties would agree metrics for tracking the SLA. The success consultant might recommend that bonus plans in marketing be changed to include deals done, not just leads generated. Sales would then feel marketing has more skin in the game.

And this would lead to achievement of the success outcome. That in turn would open opportunities for more revenue for the marketing automation vendor from this customer and from referrals. And note the success consultant isn't working on the marketing automation software or its direct benefits. He or she is working on the bigger requirements to achieve the success outcome. So, the customer will be happy to pay for his/her time.

Project Outcome Measures

Generation 3 vendors have evolved the way they drive projects. A successful go-live doesn't constitute project success. They know they must enable or improve the success outcome. As a result, they:

- set measurable objectives at the start of a project
- change their project-management techniques to focus on achieving those objectives
- measure the results achieved
- feedback the results to the customer executives who sponsored the project

Some projects are small and ad-hoc and don't need this approach. But Generation 3 vendors manage any sizeable project to deliver real and measurable improvements in the success outcome.

New Relic is a Digital Performance Monitoring and Management company. They're experts at measurement. Greg Taylor, Group Vice President, APAC, said:

We measure at all levels. We track usage closely, both number of users and usage of key features. Our most important internal measure is Monthly Active Users.

For product outcomes, we use our products to give insight into the customers' technical environments. For example, we can identify potential duplications between applications. The customer reduces cost by eliminating one or more duplicate functions.

On success outcomes, a good example is a large telco. They were changing their development approach and wanted to know how effective the new approach was. We showed them how to set up measures to give them insight into the efficiency of delivery compared to the previous waterfall method.

On project success, a good example is a customer moving to the Cloud. This is a project in itself. We help them track the ROI achieved by this move as well as impacts on measures like customer experience and satisfaction.

Monitoring the Lifecycle

Generation 3 vendors have metrics for each step of their customer lifecycle. They check effectiveness of each step. The metrics help identify where corrective action can improve results.

Deputy is a workforce management solution for casual and permanent workers, providing businesses of any size with optimised rosters, time and attendance, communication and compliance solutions suitable to any industry. They have a well-refined approach to monitoring their customer lifecycle. Ashik Ahmed, the CEO, CTO and Co-founder, said:

We monitor our customer lifecycle based on their user journey with Deputy. This begins right from when they visit our website, and convert to sign up, and continue to follow the customer's engagement throughout the trial period. We continue monitoring the sign-up cohorts from week 1 through to becoming a paying customer. Once they are a paying customer, we monitor their usage of key features within the product, which is a key indicator of engagement and retention. For example, we've discovered that people who upload their photo have a higher likelihood of remaining an active user. We also follow our Net Promoter Score very closely—it is one of our most important performance indicators—as well as our Annual/Monthly Run Rate, so we can really see what's happening at every stage of the cycle.

> **Generation 3 vendors productise as much of the success outcome as possible.**
>
> ---
>
> There's always a gap between the product outcome and the success outcome.
>
> Generation 3 vendors with low complexity offerings and low touch models productise almost everything required for the success outcome.
>
> Generation 3 vendors with high complexity offerings and high touch models rely on services and consulting to bridge the outcome gap. But they expand the use of products to do so.

Products vs Consulting and Services

For most customers, there's a gap between the vendor's product outcome and the customer's success outcome (see Fig 17 on the following page).

Generation 3 vendors make the gap as small as possible. But how do they make the gap small? If the vendor's offering is complex, it's likely to be through consulting and services.

The success outcome will have many aspects outside the vendor's control. For example, an ERP software vendor's success outcome may be Operational Effectiveness. The ERP system is critical but not sufficient.

Fig 17: There's a gap between product and success outcomes

There are processes to design, people skills to develop and partners to bring into the fold. Change management affects the success. As does the level of involvement of customer executives.

For complex offerings, Generation 3 vendors provide Success Consultants. They guide the customer on most aspects required to achieve the success outcome.

For vendors with simpler offerings, particularly lower priced offerings, the customers won't pay for consulting and services. These Generation 3 vendors bridge the outcome gap with products.

Deputy is a workforce management solution for shift-based workers, providing businesses of any size with optimised rosters, time and attendance, communication and compliance solutions suitable to any industry. Ashik Ahmed, Deputy's CEO, CTO and Co-founder, saw the need to productise the outcome gap from the company's beginning. In addition to their core offering, they've productised their onboarding with:

- *WalkMe*—helps users navigate the features of web-based services using pop-up tip balloons
- *Optimizely*—customer experience optimisation
- *FullStory*—track and improve website interaction
- *ClearBit*—captures additional data to enrich sign-ups, identify prospects and gain customer insight

- *Intercom*—chat with prospective and existing customers within an app, on a website, through social media, or via email
- *Delighted*—instant tracking of Net Promoter Score

Deputy aims to achieve maximum customer success with the least effort by customers.

The amount of time a vendor can invest with each customer also affects how the vendor bridges the outcome gap. In the book *Customer Success* (Dasteel, 2016), the authors discuss high touch, low touch and tech touch customers. They provide insight into dealing with each group. The construct of high touch, low touch and tech touch helps when considering the degree of productisation required.

In bridging the outcome gap, vendors spend more one-on-one time with their high touch customers, less with their low touch customers and very little with tech touch customers. Productisation increases in importance as the degree of touch decreases.

So, we have complexity and touch as two key factors affecting the need for productisation. We can illustrate how that looks:

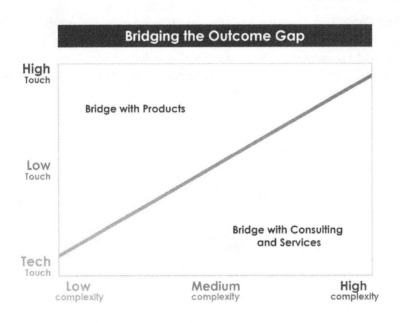

Fig 18: Bridging the outcome gap

Trouble Spots

For vendors of complex offerings, their tech touch and some of their low touch customers will struggle. These customers don't have the in-house skills to bridge the outcome gap by themselves and can't afford to pay for consulting. Consequently, they find it difficult to achieve their success outcome.

Other areas of risk also exist. For vendors of complex offerings, a lack of success consulting will reduce the chance of the customer achieving the success outcome. Some customers have all the in-house expertise needed. But many customers aren't experts in achieving the success outcome. They benefit from the vendor having this expertise. If it's not available, the risk of failure increases. And this puts the vendor's revenue at risk.

Another trouble spot occurs where vendors with offerings of low complexity (and presumably lower cost) don't productise onboarding. Their customers will struggle, again increasing the risk to the vendor's revenue.

Make Everything Simpler

Ashik Ahmed of Deputy believes everything can be made simple. And it's the obligation of vendors to do so. Simplification can be achieved by increasing the amount of productisation in bridging the outcome gap. Using the same diagram, on the following page, we see this happening:

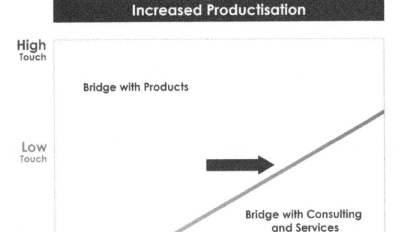

Fig 19: Productise the outcome gap

Generation 3 vendors all understand they must focus on the success outcome and help the customer bridge the gap. Some focus on productisation of the gap, others bridge it with consulting and services. But it's clear that, over time, more and more of the bridging will come from products.

PART 3
NEW BUSINESS SALES

> **Generation 3 vendors sell their ability to deliver a to-be state or success outcome.**
>
> ---
>
> They continue to use existing sales methodologies for new business.
>
> Generation 1 vendors (Features Generation) sold new business by showing they met the customers' requirements better than other vendors.
>
> Generation 2 vendors (Solution Generation) solve current problems. They sell solutions. They use one of the many solution-selling methodologies.
>
> Generation 3 vendors (Outcome Generation) continue to use many of the techniques from solution-selling. But they focus on enabling a success outcome, not only on solving current problems.
>
> Generation 3 vendors sell the dream. But they understand they need to earn the right to do that.
>
> When the outcome gap is large, differences in product features make less difference.

For clarity, we're talking here about sales to an organisation with which a vendor has no established relationship. They're sometimes referred to as *Net New* or *New Logo* sales.

For existing customers, Generation 3 Customer Success involves a joint planning process. Joint planning requires an established relationship. In new business sales, there's no established relationship. The vendor wants to establish that relationship by winning the initial deal.

In new business sales, vendors need a different sales process from the one for existing customers. Great methodologies have emerged over the years, including Solution Selling, Strategic Selling, SPIN Selling, Target Account Selling and more recently, The Challenger Sale. All provide a structure, processes and guidelines on how to prosecute complex sales. The good news is that Generation 3 vendors still use their current methodology.

How they sell new business deals doesn't change much. It's what they sell that changes.

How Generations 1 and 2 Sell New Business Deals

Generation 1 vendors show how they meet the prospect's requirements. They respond, feature by feature, to the long checklists in the prospect's requirements documents. Vendors conduct lengthy demonstrations, hoping to gain more ticks in the spreadsheet than competitors. This approach dates all the way back to the 1970s, when software packages first appeared. For the vendor and the prospect, the process can best be described as agonising.

The reason it's agonising is simple. It requires focus on something the buyer doesn't care about—the vendor's products and services. Buyers care about the outcome they want to achieve. While they know the products and services are a means to that end, they're mostly interested in the end result, or outcome. But the Generation 1 approach forces vendors to talk about their products. For prospects, it's boring—mind-numbingly boring.

Few commercial organisations buy this way anymore. But many regulated organisations such as government must still use this approach.

In the late '80s and early '90s, Generation 2 took over. There were sighs of relief from vendors and prospects alike. The impetus came from Generation 2 vendors, who realised that competing using a Generation 1 approach was too hard. The checklist approach produced a lottery—anyone might win. And sometimes the lotteries weren't fair. If someone in the prospect wanted one vendor to win, they based their requirements document on the vendor's product. The preferred vendor nearly always won.

Generation 2 vendors took a different approach. They asked to visit the customer's business in person. The vendors wanted to understand the business and its problems first-hand. With that first-hand knowledge they'd then apply experience solving similar problems in other customers. They told the prospects they could thus develop a better solution to the problems.

In the early days of Generation 2, prospects often resisted. They didn't want vendors talking to line management. The IT department wanted to control everything, including access. The prospects warned vendors if they approached management directly, exclusion from the selection process would result.

Generation 2 vendors persisted. They brought a new breed of consultant to the pre-sales process. Generation 1 pre-sales consultants were product experts. They knew the detail of the product and they impressed prospects with their depth of knowledge.

Generation 2 pre-sales consultants had an extra skill. Not only did they have expertise in the software, they became experts in solving the customers' problems. And the best of these consultants wouldn't need to be told a prospect's problems. They'd win credibility by asking the prospect if they had a particular set of problems. Because the consultants knew the prospect's industry well, they usually got it right. This hooked the prospect. The prospect assumed that if these consultants knew the problems they faced, the vendor must have a solution.

Generation 2 ushered in the era of solution-selling. More than a quarter of a century later, solution-selling still dominates the industry. That's quite remarkable given the speed at which everything else in the technology industry changes.

New Business Deals Have Changed

Subscription pricing changes everything for technology vendors. They have never previously had a compelling financial reason to ensure customer success. Now they have.

With perpetual licences and project-based services, the vendor received most of the revenue early. The customer paid for software licences upfront, then paid for services as implementation progressed. By the time the vendor finished the implementation, they had most of the revenue they'd get over the first three to five years.

With subscription pricing, the customers invest less in the early years. If an implementation isn't a success, it's less costly to drop the vendor. Of course, the internal disruption of starting a new project with a different vendor shouldn't be underestimated. But for many customers who haven't enjoyed the success they expected, the disruption is worth it. Most vendors have experienced the anger of customers who failed to achieve success.

Subscription-pricing vendors face a bigger issue—usage. If the customer isn't successful, their usage doesn't grow. And that has a big impact for the vendor's revenue. In the past, traditional vendors sold the licences the prospect might need for the first two or three years. The licences would sit, waiting for usage to increase. The term shelfware emerged for these licences-in-waiting.

With subscription pricing, customers don't buy everything upfront. They buy the smallest number of users possible. They know that as usage increases, they will need more users. But they don't want to pay until they're needed.

The vendor hopes everything will go smoothly and usage will quickly increase. But that doesn't always happen. A delay in an implementation will delay increased usage. A lack of success in the project will cause usage to stagnate. Or even drop. In each of these cases, the vendor takes a financial hit. The potential revenue loss provides a significant incentive for the vendor to ensure customer success.

Before subscription pricing, new-business sales teams focused on the initial deal. They'd joke that implementation was a post-sales issue. With subscription pricing, the 'sale' never stops. Customer success should lead to increasing revenue. But if success doesn't occur, revenue will remain flat or reduce. The initial sale is no longer a 'big win'. Now, it establishes the relationship. And sets the scene for growth only if the customer enjoys success.

Subscription-pricing new-business sales teams understand they need to set the relationship and the initial project up in a new way. They can't just focus on the initial deal. They must maximise the chance of increasing revenue over time. Generation 2 subscription-pricing vendors focus on ensuring the customer has success with their products and services. But as we've discussed, product outcomes aren't the end-result. The prospect wants to achieve a success outcome, not a product outcome.

Generation 3 vendors have learned to sell something bigger than a product outcome.

Generation 3 Vendors Sell the Dream

Generation 3 vendors don't sell product outcomes. They sell a to-be state. They help the prospect envisage a new to-be state, then show the prospect how to achieve that to-be state.

To provide a simple example, think of a travel agent. When you walk into a travel agent, the posters on the wall show relaxed people sitting on golden beaches sipping a cool drink or swooshing down a snow-covered mountain or wandering the streets of exotic cities. The posters depict the to-be state. People can envisage themselves in the scenes on the travel posters.

Of course, what the travel agent does is find flights, arrange transfers, arrange hotels, obtain visas, provide insurance and so on. But they never mention that in the posters. They sell the dream of sitting on a golden beach sipping a cool drink. That's the to-be state the customer wants, so that's what they sell.

Generation 3 vendors do the same thing. They develop a to-be state the customer will find appealing and they sell the dream.

Earning the Right to Sell the Dream

The marketing messages from Generation 3 vendors focus on the success outcome the vendor serves. If the vendor has chosen their success outcome well, it will resonate with the target market. When key executives hear the message, it should create a mental picture of a to-be state. And a good percentage of them should think, 'I want that'. To continue the travel poster analogy, they can see themselves on the ski slope or relaxing on a golden beach. And they want to be in that picture. When this occurs, the Generation 3 vendor has already won the right to sell the dream—the to-be state they can help the prospect achieve.

But in lots of sales situations, the vendor's contact with the prospect begins much later in the prospect's buying process. The prospect has already moved a long way through their buying process. The team from CEB, in their *Challenger Sale* series (Dixon M. a., 2011), (Adamson, 2015), suggest this occurs 57% of the way into the prospect's buying process.

When this occurs, Generation 3 vendors sell differently. If the prospect has a Generation 1 buying process planned, the vendor must first give confidence they can meet the requirements. If the prospect has a Generation 2 buying process, the vendor must give confidence they have a solution to the prospect's problems. In both cases, the prospect's confidence doesn't have to reach 100%. It just has to be high enough to make the Generation 3 vendor a contender for the deal.

Once the prospect has enough confidence, the Generation 3 vendor moves the prospect's thinking towards a possible new to-be state. Again, borrowing from the work of CEB, this is where they offer Commercial Insight. And it centres around imbuing the prospect with a vision of a new to-be state. Achieving the to-be state will solve the prospect's problems. But it will also do more than just solve current problems. The focus of the Generation 3 vendor's sales process is the desirability of the success outcome and why they can best enable it for the prospect.

Gen 3 Vendors Make Strong Emotional Connections

Buying has two steps—making an emotional decision to buy, then rationalising that decision. Buying technology products and services isn't different. The prospect first makes an emotional commitment to one vendor, then comes up with good reasons to support that choice.

There's always a success outcome the prospect wants to achieve. There's a reason they've decided to spend money on IT. Someone has decided they'll be better off. And prospects don't care about a vendor's products and services. These are just a means to an end. The prospect has a bigger outcome they want to achieve—the success outcome.

As a result, vendors whose sales process focuses on their products and services make a weak emotional link with the prospect. Vendors who show they can solve the current problems make a stronger emotional connection. But Generation 3 vendors go further. They sell their ability to enable the success outcome. They appeal directly to the thing the customer cares about most—getting the outcome they really want. This creates a much deeper emotional connection.

Establishing the strongest emotional connection produces the greatest likelihood of winning the deal. The prospect will always find a way to rationalise and justify their choice.

Qualifying Leads

Generation 2 emerged as a way for vendors to compete on a new basis. Their products had matured, so the differences in features and functions weren't enough as a differentiator. They wanted to compete on their ability to deliver a solution to a set of problems. They hated Generation 1 sales deals.

They knew if a prospect wanted to follow a Generation 1 approach, the chances of winning were small. So, unless the prospect was an organisation such as government required to follow a Generation 1 approach, they qualified out.

Now, most vendors are capable Generation 2 vendors. They know how to analyse problems and develop a solution. For vendors in mature markets, the ability to differentiate their solution has grown more and more difficult.

Gen 3 vendors sell a to-be state or success outcome, not a product outcome. They're finding that, if a prospect wants to follow a Gen 2 approach, they may be better off qualifying out. It's better to find prospects who love a success outcome, not compete for a Gen 2 deal anyone can win.

Relative (Un)Importance of Product in New Business

Product-based technology vendors love their products. They love adding new features and functions. And when they do, they love telling everyone about the great new features.

But for new-business sales, how important are product features?

Prospects want to achieve a success outcome. Even if they haven't verbalised it this way, they know there's a lot more to a successful project than the things provided by a vendor. We've already discussed the relationship between product outcomes and success outcomes.

Fig 20: Relationship between product and success outcomes

Let's look at achievement of the success outcome. For the sake of this example, assume half of the achievement comes from the vendor's offering (the product outcome). The other half comes from things the customer does themselves, such as change management and decisions on processes, staffing, policies, etc.

Now let's consider the product outcome. Let's assume half of the product outcome comes from the product's functionality and half from the quality of the implementation.

So, half of the achievement of the success outcome comes from the product outcome, and half of the product outcome comes from the product functionality. So only one quarter (25%) of the success outcome comes from the product functionality.

Fig 21: Product is a small part of the success outcome

Let's say a vendor has a superior product that has 10% more functionality than its competitors. The vendor assumes a gap of that size will result in the prospect choosing them. Their sales pitch focuses on the benefits that will flow from this extra 10% of functionality. But they're disappointed and frustrated when the prospect isn't excited by this 10% gap.

The prospect isn't excited by that product gap because in their mind, product contributes only 25% to the success outcome. A 10% gap in product translates to only a 2.5% difference to success. It's not significant in the prospect's mind.

Now consider how a Generation 3 vendor competes for the same business. They position their product as comparable to the competitors. And then they stop talking about the product. They focus on the things required for success that aren't part of the product outcome. They show they understand everything the customer needs for success, and they can help with most of it.

Vendors still need a product that's comparable to the competition. It's the price of entry. A product that's too far behind won't be given a chance to compete. But Generation 3 vendors have learned that product functionality doesn't win deals.

In our example, half of the success outcome comes from the product outcome and half from the other elements—things the customer does themselves. Generation 3 vendors have learned they can do more to differentiate by helping with this 'other' half. And the larger the gap between product outcome and success outcome, the better it is to focus on bridging the gap and not on product. And that's how Generation 3 vendors win.

PART 4
GENERATION 3 CUSTOMER LOYALTY

> The more of a success outcome provided by a vendor, the higher the loyalty. Provided the customer experience is acceptable.
>
> ---
>
> There's a difference between loyalty and lock-in.
>
> Loyalty is a combination of what a vendor provides and how well it is delivered.
>
> What a vendor provides should enable the success outcome. The more of the success outcome provided, the higher the loyalty.
>
> Good customer experience is the price of entry to the technology market. If it's good, loyalty will be neutral.
>
> Extraordinary loyalty requires an extra element—a new and much-loved success outcome.

Loyalty vs Lock-in

Let's consider two different types of loyalty programs. In *Customer Success* (Mehta, 2016), Nick Mehta, Dan Steinman and Lincoln Murphy describe this difference:

> *Much has been written about different kinds of loyalty. There are two kinds of loyalty—attitudinal loyalty and behavioural loyalty. These are sometime referred to as emotional loyalty and intellectual loyalty.*

This distinction helps. For some companies or products, we want to work with them. There's a positive emotional link. For other companies or products, we work with them despite our ambivalence or even antipathy. There's no positive emotional link.

The *Oxford Dictionary* defines loyalty as 'a strong feeling of support or allegiance'. If we apply that definition, it seems that attitudinal loyalty fits best. Given this, and with deference to the authors of *Customer Success*, I'd like to bring their insights into even starker contrast—let's call the two states loyalty and lock-in.

Customers who feel loyalty want to work with that company or product. They forgive imperfections. They advocate the virtues of the company or product. There'd have to be a huge advantage in a competitor's offering before they'd switch.

Apple provides the perennial example. The authors of *Customer Success* say, 'Steve Jobs figured out how to create attitudinal loyalty perhaps better than anyone, before or since. And it's literally priceless.'

In contrast, we also have companies or products we continue to use even though we don't much like them. We continue because the cost or difficulty of changing is high, or we lose some benefit if we change. We're locked into using that company or product.

Airline loyalty programs provide an example. Many people feel locked-in. They want to accumulate points, so they stay with an airline. But the program doesn't make them feel positively toward that airline. After all, most airlines offer the same sort of program. But customers know they'll lose benefits if they don't use that airline. They feel locked-in. They continue to use the airline, but without 'a strong feeling of support or allegiance.' In some cases, the 'locked-in' feeling can even breed resentment.

How does this idea link to customer success? The authors of *Customer Success* say, 'Customer Success is designed to create attitudinal loyalty'. Generation 3 vendors could not agree more, and they believe enabling a success outcome is key. After all, customers don't care about the vendor's products or services. Customers care about the success outcome they want to achieve. The success outcome describes a to-be state the customer wants. It has meaning and connection for the customer. If a vendor enables the to-be state, they create a strong emotional connection. They engender loyalty.

Generation 3 Loyalty Elements

Now let's consider loyalty. Achieving loyal customers has two elements. First, what's offered. Second, how it's delivered.

What's Provided

The concept is simple. The higher the percentage of the customer's success outcome provided, the greater the loyalty. The customer cares about the success outcome. When they achieve their success outcome, they feel great. The more of the success outcome provided by a vendor, the more the positive emotion transfers to the vendor. This creates loyalty. It creates 'a strong feeling of support or allegiance'.

In Figure 22, Vendor B delivers much more of what's needed to achieve the success outcome the customer wants. The customer will feel much greater loyalty to Vendor B than to Vendor A.

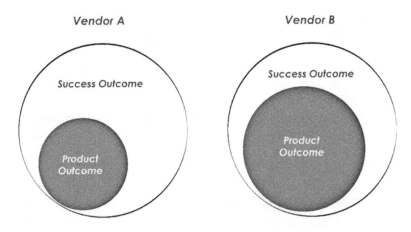

Fig 22: The success outcome drives loyalty

Let's continue with the example of Apple. iPhones offer both business and personal connection. For business, there's email, online storage, business applications, videoconferencing and of course phone calls. For personal, there's music, videos, social media and lots of personal apps. A possible success outcome the iPhone serves (the to-be state it creates) is 'personal and business connected'. And the iPhone does most of what's needed for that success outcome. So, it creates a strong emotional connection—loyalty.

How the Vendor Delivers Their Offering

The second loyalty element considers how a vendor delivers their offering. We can capture the delivery concept in a single phrase—customer experience. Generation 3 vendors have learned that a good customer experience is the price of entry to the market. If the customer experience isn't good, the vendor will lose customers. But they've also learned that having a good customer experience doesn't guarantee customers' loyalty. The customers know other vendors offer the same or even better customer experience.

In *The Effortless Experience* (Dixon M. T., 2013), another great book by CEB, Matthew Dixon, Nicholas Toman and Rick DeLisi offer four

103

findings about customer experience, seen through the lens of the customer service function:

Finding # 1: A Strategy of Delight Doesn't Pay

While leaders clearly believe in the power of exceeding customer expectations in building customer loyalty, the data tells a different story. As we analyse responses from more than 97,000 customers, what we find is that there is virtually no difference at all between loyalty of those customers whose expectations are exceeded and those whose expectations are simply met... Rather than a 'hockey stick effect'—where loyalty skyrockets upward—loyalty actually plateaus once customer expectations are met.

Finding #2: Satisfaction Is Not a Predictor of Loyalty

In our global survey, we found virtually no statistical relationship between how a customer rates a company on a satisfaction survey and their future customer loyalty.

Finding # 3: Customer Service Interactions Tend to Drive Disloyalty, Not Loyalty

Most companies often don't even meet customer expectations, so the result is that most customers end up more disloyal to our companies than before...

Finding #4: The Key to Mitigating Disloyalty is Reducing Customer Effort

Generation 3 vendors have learned similar lessons. They've learned that exceeding expectations (in effect, surprising the customer) isn't sustainable. They don't try to do that. They've learned not to use customer satisfaction surveys that are product-outcome focused. They know they need to focus on success outcomes.

They've learned that Generation 3 Customer Success is a joint effort between the vendor and customer. Both need to plan together and execute together. Both sides then deliver what's expected of them in enabling the success outcome. And the vendor needs to ensure the customer experience in this mutual engagement is a positive one.

Generation 3 vendors know they must deliver a minimum standard for the customer experience. If they achieve that standard, there's a neutral effect on loyalty. If they fall below the standard, loyalty will decline. And they know it's extremely difficult to get an increase in loyalty from customer experience alone.

Putting the Two Elements Together

Strong loyalty comes from:

- providing most of what the customer needs to achieve their success outcome, and
- delivering it with a positive customer experience

Net Promoter Score

The Net Promoter Score is a widely used tool for estimating customer loyalty. Here's a description from Shep Hyken (Hyken, 2016):

On a scale of zero to 10, with 10 being highest, what's the likelihood that you would recommend us (our company) to a friend or colleague?

That is the basic Net Promoter Score (also known as NPS) question that was created by Fred Reicheld and Bain & Company. I've always found it to be powerful survey question to determine overall customer sentiment. Did the company, or whomever the customer was interacting with, do a good enough job to garner a nine or a 10?

The score, on a scale of one to 10, falls into three groups. If a customer scores you as a nine or a 10, they are promoters. If they score you as a seven or an eight, they are passive. You don't know if they are leaning toward loving you, leaving you, or they just don't care. And, a score of a six or lower means you have a detractor. To determine your official NPS score, take the percentage of promoters (nines and 10s) and subtract the percentage of detractors (sixes and lower). That number is your Net Promoter Score.

Companies usually ask qualitative questions as well. From the same article by Shep Hyken:

My experience is that most customers will take the short NPS survey. They may even answer another question or two. Two of my favorite questions to follow the standard one-to-10 survey are to ask, 'Why?' and if the number is lower than a 10, 'What would it take to raise our score just by one point?' In other words, go from a six to a seven, or a nine to a 10. That is important feedback that any company can use.

Scoring Generation 3 Loyalty

It's possible to use the two elements of Gen 3 customer loyalty (what's provided and how it's delivered) to create a customer loyalty score. But given the popularity of NPS, why bother?

The reason—Generation 3 loyalty provides a different insight. The NPS score gives an indication of intention to recommend. But a low NPS score doesn't lead to any conclusions about corrective action. The vendor's management will need to work that out themselves. Hopefully, they've asked open-ended questions and customers have given enough detail to indicate where the problems lie.

For Generation 3 vendors, there's a structure for considering how to improve loyalty. If a customer experience score is low, the vendor can address that. Myriad books, videos and consultants are available to help. If the percentage of the success outcome provided is low, the vendor can provide more of what's needed. And increasing the percentage of the success outcome provided not only increases loyalty, it increases revenue.

The second advantage of using Generation 3 loyalty is in creativity of solutions. With NPS, a vendor asks customers open-ended questions about the score they give. If the customer scores the vendor low, the customer's reasons will focus on what's wrong with the current products and services. But Generation 3 vendors don't focus on current problems. They enable a new to-be state for customers. They solve the current problems as a by-product of enabling the new to-be state. And, using the thinking from *The Challenger Customer* (Adamson, 2015), vendors need to provide new commercial insight. They need to provide new ways of looking at the customer's business. The to-be state creates new opportunities for the customer if developed creatively.

Generation 3 vendors measure both customer experience and percentage of success outcome provided. They never ignore the feedback provided as part of the NPS process. But they also don't limit their thinking to solving the problems captured through this feedback.

Calculating Generation 3 Loyalty

To create an overall score, we calculate and combine both elements of Generation 3 loyalty.

What's Provided

Consider all the things the customer requires to achieve their success outcome. Then calculate the percentage of those things provided by the vendor. That's the success outcome score.

How the Vendor Delivers the Offering

A good customer experience (comparable to the competitors) scores 1.0 on the customer experience scale. The loyalty score doesn't go up or down. If the customer experience isn't good enough, it will score below 1.0. If it's exceptionally good, it may go above 1.0, but is unlikely to exceed 1.2. This is the customer experience score.

Customer Loyalty Score

The customer loyalty score is the success outcome score multiplied by the customer experience score. If a vendor scored 80% on success outcome and 1.0 on customer experience, they score 80% on customer loyalty. If a vendor scored 60% on customer success and 0.75 on customer experience, they score 45% on customer loyalty.

The equation:

Loyalty (LTY) = percentage of customer success provided (%SO) multiplied by the customer experience score (CX):

$$LTY = \%SO \times CX$$

Vendors can't score loyalty by themselves. For Generation 3 vendors, customers provide the score. In the end, the vendor's trying to assess their customer's emotional state—how the customer feels about them.

Extraordinary Loyalty

Everyone has admired the loyalty Apple has created for the iPhone and iPad. Let's consider the success outcome served by these products.

They connect us to personal things we like—music, social media, apps, news, directions and so on. They also connect us to business things we need—business apps, our contacts, to-do lists, calendar, email and other communication and collaboration tools.

A possible success outcome served by these Apple products is 'personal and business connected'.

The Generation 3 loyalty theory suggests the high loyalty comes from the delivery of most of the success outcome. If 'personal and business connected' is correct as the iPhone/iPad's success outcome, they indeed offer most of what we need.

But in Apple's case, there's something more to this loyalty. We've marvelled at the lines of people outside Apple Stores waiting to buy the latest device.

What created this extraordinary loyalty?

Here's a possibility. The extraordinary loyalty started because the success outcome of 'personal and business connected' was new and unexpected. And people loved this new success outcome.

Apple completed the picture by delivering almost everything needed to achieve the new success outcome. The extraordinary loyalty came from a combination of creating a new and loved success outcome and then delivering most of it.

Given this, we can add a third element to the Loyalty calculation— the uniqueness and attraction of a success outcome. If it's new and customers love it, loyalty will increase.

For scoring, let's assume a poorly chosen success outcome will reduce loyalty to a vendor. A good success outcome will be neutral on loyalty. A new and well-loved success outcome will increase loyalty. The range might be 0.5 to 1.5. Let's call this the 'love factor'.

The formula would now be as follows:

Loyalty (LTY) = the love factor for the success outcome (♥ SO) multiplied by percentage of customer success provided (%SO) multiplied by the customer experience score (CX):

$$LTY = ♥ SO \times \%SO \times CX$$

Summary

Loyalty has three elements:

- how much the customers love the success outcome you serve
- how much of this success outcome you provide
- how well you deliver it (customer experience)

PART 5
IMPLEMENTING GENERATION 3 CUSTOMER SUCCESS

Generation 3 provides a framework.

Each vendor will develop a customer success program tailored to their unique business.

There are six steps to Generation 3 Customer Success.

Fig 23: The six steps to Generation 3 Customer Success

113

Step 1 — Define the Success Outcome

Generation 3 Technology Vendors have scope to choose a success outcome that makes sense for their business.

Vendors should choose a success outcome they will serve. There is considerable latitude in the outcome definition they choose.

The success outcome must pass the significance squared test. The vendor must be significant for the success outcome and the outcome must be significant to the customer.

Defining a Vendor's Success Outcome

Most technology vendors have some area of specialty, or a unique combination of products and services. That specialty will influence the success outcome they choose to serve. But the choice is not automatic. There is as much art as science in the choice.

An outcome is a to-be state. It describes something the customer wants to achieve. Generation 3 vendors use two methods to generate ideas on the success outcome they serve. First, list the problems the customers face. Identify the top three. Then, describe the to-be state the customer would enjoy if they eliminated those top three problems.

The second method is for a vendor to ask themselves, 'If a customer made perfect use of my products or services and if they followed my advice exactly, how would I describe the state I helped create for the customer?'

Let's illustrate this second approach. We'll start with ERP software. ERP software automates business operations. What if a customer made perfect use of an ERP system and followed the vendor's advice exactly? The customer's operations would run at peak efficiency and effectiveness. The success outcome an ERP vendor serves could be 'effective operations' or 'optimised operations' or 'operating costs minimised'.

How about CRM software? A wide variety of possibilities exist for this genre. If a customer used CRM software perfectly and followed vendor advice they would have a sales team with a strong process, they would capture knowledge about customers and they'd have great insight into their own funnel or pipeline. The success outcome could be something like 'disciplined sales team' or 'informed forecast'.

Now consider marketing automation. The success outcome served by marketing automation vendors could be 'pipeline generated'. If the customer uses the system to maintain relationships, the success outcome could be 'prospects and customers nurtured'.

Content management—the success outcome could be 'information and history accessible' or 'informed and governed decisions'.

It's clear that even within the same genre, quite different success outcomes could be chosen. Vendors will have expertise or products that would cause them to lean in one direction or another. Part of the thinking should be how they would differentiate from and gain a competitive advantage over other vendors in the genre. Variations of the success outcome would allow them to do so.

Vendors can apply some tests and guidelines to refine and finalise their success outcome.

Knowing the Problems Solved

Enabling a success outcome solves customer problems. Solving the problems is a by-product of achieving the success outcome. Generation 3 vendors know the problems their success outcome solves. They can articulate those problems and how their success outcome solves them. They assess the size of those problems when choosing a success outcome.

Significance Squared Test

The ultimate success outcome for a customer might be financial results achieved or return to shareholders. A technology vendor might be tempted to say that's the success outcome they serve.

In theory this is true, but in practice it doesn't help. The impact an individual technology vendor will have on overall financial results is small.

Here's what that would look like:

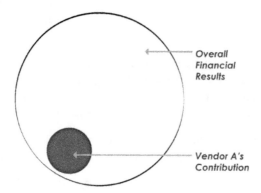

Fig 24: Vendor's contribution to results is insignificant

The vendor needs a Goldilocks test. The term refers to the fairy tale in which Goldilocks tastes porridge. The first bowl of porridge was too hot, the second too cold, but the third was just right. Vendors need a test like this to choose a success outcome definition that is just right, not too big and not too small.

The Goldilocks test is how significant the vendor is for the success outcome. If a vendor isn't significant for a success outcome, the customer won't pay attention to anything they say. To illustrate, a CEO is unlikely to consult a CRM vendor on how to improve overall profitability.

Success outcomes nest. The largest success outcome (financial results) has smaller success outcomes that contribute to it. These, in turn, have smaller success outcomes. The vendor should choose a success outcome for which they're significant. It will be a subset of the overall outcome the customer must achieve.

Here's what that would look like:

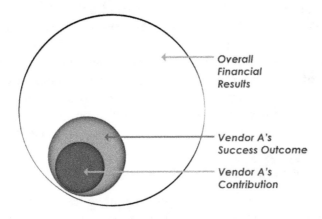

Overall
Financial
Results

Vendor A's
Success Outcome

Vendor A's
Contribution

Fig 25: The vendor must be significant

For this outcome, the vendor is significant. It means when the vendor engages with the customer's staff who look after this outcome, the vendor will be important to those staff.

The question would then be how to measure significance. Simply, the vendor should provide the largest share of the products or services for the success outcome. The share does not have to exceed 50%, but it must be larger than any other vendor. Note that the customer does some of the activities themselves. The vendor doesn't have to provide more than the customer, just more than any other supplier.

There's a second aspect to the significance test. The customer must want the outcome you've defined. If the customer doesn't care about the success outcome you've chosen, then your outcome won't drive business. For example, a marketing automation vendor might choose 'prospects nurtured' as their success outcome. But if no-one understood the concept or was interested in nurturing, the vendor would not attract customers.

So, the significance squared test has two aspects. First, the vendor must play a significant role in delivering the success outcome. Second, the success outcome must be significant to the intended customer. If either test fails, then the chosen success outcome fails.

Unique vs Market-matching Success Outcomes

As discussed, choosing the success outcome isn't a science. As well as the question of significance, there's also the question of how unique the success outcome should be. Some vendors will choose a success outcome different from any competitor. They'll then build a unique portfolio of products and services. These vendors compete on having a more attractive success outcome. Other vendors will match the competitors' success outcome but develop stronger execution. They compete on being able to enable a success outcome better than anyone else.

Single-step or Two-step Success Outcome

Vendors that serve business end-users have a single step. Their success outcome is that of the end-users they serve. To illustrate, ERP software is used directly by business end-users. The success outcome of 'effective operations' reflects the needs of these business end-users.

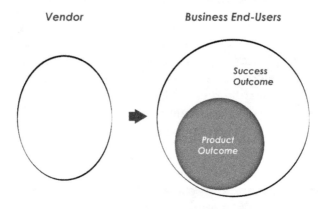

Fig 26: Single-step success outcome

Other vendors don't directly serve business end-users. These include:

- vendors who provide products for support departments such as HR departments, Support departments,
- vendors who provide enabling technology such as database, performance management
- managed-service providers
- vendors who sell through partners

These vendors serve two success outcomes. They appreciate the success outcome of the business end-users and are clear about how they help enable that success outcome. But the business end-users will probably not be the decision-makers when choosing a vendor. The decision-makers will be the support departments such as HR or Support, or the IT department for technology vendors. These vendors appreciate the decision-makers must also get a win. For vendors who serve two-step success outcomes, the relationship is shown in Figure 27.

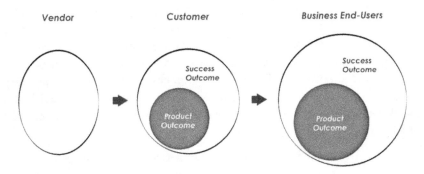

Fig 27: A two-step success outcome

Multiple Lines of Business

Vendors may have more than one line of business. Each line of business requires a separate success outcome. It's possible for a vendor to serve a success outcome with two elements. If they believe they have three or more elements, it's likely they have more than one line of business.

10-syllable Rule

Generation 3 vendors describe their success outcomes succinctly. They need to create an image, a clear idea of the to-be state the customer wants. The success outcome should capture the imagination of the customer. Generation 3 vendors have learned to capture the success outcome in two or three words. They don't use a lengthy sentence. They also don't include any jargon or technical wording—the words make sense to business end-users. Generation 3 vendors have learned to describe the success outcome they serve in 10 syllables or fewer.

Generation 3 Vendors Don't Ask the Customer, At First

A technology vendor considering the success outcome they serve might be tempted to ask the customer. While the customer must eventually agree with the success outcome, asking them upfront isn't the right timing.

Apple didn't ask the customers first when developing the iPhone and iPod. Apple worked out what the customers really needed, and then showed them.

And Generation 3 vendors learned they need to think differently about themselves. They want the customer to see them as a contributor to the success outcome and not just a provider of a product or service. Part of the journey means coming to grips with that change themselves. Before they can convince the customer, they must change their own thinking. They need to break the mould and see themselves as something more than just a provider of the current products or services.

That's what Generation 3 thinking can do—allow vendors to see themselves in a different light. By breaking the constraints of their own thinking, they can generate new ideas for growth and develop new relationships with customers.

Other Questions

Before they're ready to talk with customers, Generation 3 vendors ask themselves other questions about possible success outcomes they can serve:

- Will the success outcome give us a competitive advantage? Can we look different from and better than competitors?
- How well can we enable the success outcome—do we have the products, skills, experience, etc.?
- Will customers pay to achieve the success outcome? Will improvements in the success outcome deliver large returns for the customers?

Once the vendor has chosen a success outcome, they discuss it with key customers. If they don't get a positive response, they'll start again. But they don't ask the customer before they've done their own thinking.

120

Generation 3 vendors develop a lifecycle for ideal customers and then decide their own to-be state for delivering the lifecycle.

Generation 3 vendors understand not all customers will engage using the ideal customer lifecycle.

DEEP Engagement with Ideal Customers

In Part 2, we described the ideal customer engagement model—DEEP Engagement. DEEP has four major phases—Develop, Evaluate, Execute and Prosper. These phases provide the framework around which a vendor can develop their ideal customer lifecycle. Generation 3 vendors understand not all customers will engage with them in an 'ideal' fashion. But they want as many customers as possible to convert to their ideal model over time.

To arrive at their ideal model, vendors first decide the steps in their ideal customer lifecycle.

Engagement with Other Customers

Generation 3 vendors accept that many customers won't engage using the ideal model. They need a model for these other customers. This may entail little change from the way they presently operate. But some use the lens of success outcomes to develop variations to current engagement models.

At the very least, they use metrics to identify opportunities for upsell and cross-sell. They also identify subscription or maintenance contracts due for renewal that may be under threat and take corrective action.

New Business Sales

As discussed in Part 3, Generation 3 vendors 'sell the dream'. They sell the to-be state and its benefits. As part of the to-be model, Generation 3 vendors determine how they'll sell new business deals.

Putting It Together

With an idea formed for each of these engagement groups, the vendor will have a feel for how the organisation will work and what it will look like. They'll refine this in the next steps.

Step 3 — Analyse Execution Capability

The vendor analyses what's required to achieve the desired to-be state.

The vendor conducts an execution capability analysis on the ideal customer lifecycle.

For each step in the lifecycle they identify a deliverable and KPIs for that step.

They conduct a PSPSP analysis (process, systems, people skills, partners) for each step.

They identify opportunities for improvements.

Execution Capability Analysis

We define execution capability as the underlying ability to execute a strategy. In Step 1, the vendor decided on the success outcome they would serve. This strategic decision drives activities and plans going forward.

In Step 2 — Define the To-Be State, the vendor determined the way they want to engage with existing customers and new business prospects. For most vendors, a gap will exist between the desired to-be state and the current execution capability.

In Step 3, the vendor determined the size of that gap in execution capability. For some vendors well advanced in Generation 3 Customer Success, the gap will be small and easily addressed. For others, the gap will be larger and need more effort to address.

Deliverables

At each step in the customer lifecycle, Generation 3 vendors have a deliverable to achieve. They define these deliverables clearly. These drive the behaviour of the vendor at each step in the customer lifecycle.

Many Generation 1 and 2 vendors prescribe the processes to be followed by their teams in detail. The challenge arises when the prescribed process doesn't fit a complex customer situation. A lack of flexibility in process undermines confidence and commitment to the customer lifecycle.

Generation 3 vendors provide guidance on best practices for each step of the lifecycle. But they don't insist on blind adherence. They focus on achieving the deliverable at each step. Capable teams are given the latitude to adapt the process to different customer situations.

A focus on the deliverable also fosters a continuous improvement approach by staff. The teams are encouraged to identify improved ways of achieving the deliverable.

PSPSP Analysis — Processes, Systems, People Skills and Partners

For any organisation to function, it needs processes, systems and people. Most also have partners that contribute to their execution capability. These are the four elements of execution capability.

For each step in the lifecycle, the vendor identifies the processes, systems, people skills and partners required. It's not an exhaustive analysis, it's a high-level description of what's needed for each step.

KPIs and Metrics

For each step, the vendor determines the KPIs or metrics they'll use to judge success of this step.

Opportunities for Improvement

Next, the vendor identifies gaps and records them as opportunities for improvement. It's likely the list of opportunities for improvement will be long. At this stage, that's okay. Prioritisation will take place later.

Optional Considerations

Some steps in the customer lifecycle have a greater impact on the vendor's success than others. When deciding an action plan, improvements in these steps have a higher priority.

Some steps in the lifecycle may need to vary in different regions or countries. Culture may make a different approach more effective. As part of the planning, the vendor flags any steps requiring cultural consideration.

Output

The PSPSP Analysis produces a long list of opportunities for improvement. The intent is to have an exhaustive list of everything required to bridge the execution capability gap. There'll be too many ideas to implement them all, at least at the start. In the next step, the vendor prioritises the ideas and develops a practical action plan.

Step 4 — Develop an Implementation Plan

Implementing a customer success program and evolving to Generation 3 takes time. But the rewards are worth the investment.

Implementing a customer success program is an evolution not a revolution.

Vendors should begin with customers, staff and partners who see the value of a customer success program and want to take part.

New business prospects often accept a vendor's customer success program more easily than existing customers.

Big Bang Doesn't Work

Subscription pricing has changed the industry for technology vendors. Recurring revenue is at risk. There is now a strong financial incentive to ensure customer success. Lots of vendors feel an urgency to get a program in place. They develop their program and launch it with all customers, all staff and all partners. And then they face disappointment.

The path to Generation 3 is an evolution not a revolution.

Most vendors already use aspects of Generation 3. For many, the idea of serving a success outcome won't be new, although they may not have used that term. For those vendors, the evolution will take less time.

The journey to a successful program has challenges. First, the customers won't all embrace the customer success program. Many customers have engaged with their vendors for years and have an established routine. They don't understand the need to do something different.

Second, the program may not receive universal acclaim from staff. The more progressive thinkers in the staff will see the benefits. Others, more set in their ways, will question the need for change. Some may see it as the latest fad by management. Others won't see enough personal benefit to warrant the effort.

Third, if the vendor has partners involved, they too must come along for the ride. And all partners may not be enthused.

Start with the Willing

Some customers will immediately have enthusiasm for the customer success program. If they have an IT department under pressure to enable real business results, the receptiveness will increase.

A customer success program won't work if the customers don't cooperate. As with anything new, some customers will be early adopters, some will be mainstream, and some will be laggards. Generation 3 vendors start with the early adopters. They identify the customers who need to improve results and want to work with the vendor to do so.

The same approach works with staff. Some sales team members will immediately see the potential benefits. They'll see how using Success Consultants to do high-level and detailed business case analyses will make their life easier. They know how difficult it is to compete on features and functions of the software or even on solutions to customer problems. The opportunity to create a new competitive differentiator appeals.

Other sales team members won't be enthusiastic. Many salespeople don't see beyond identifying and closing immediate opportunities. To be fair, that's often what their sales compensation plans encourage. A customer success program has strategic importance. But some salespeople may see it as an impost and believe it will slow the sales cycle. Some will see selling a business case study (10% sale) as an unnecessary step. They'd rather just try to sell the products immediately.

The leaders amongst the salespeople soon find selling business case studies easier than trying to sell products and services upfront. It brings in deals earlier as the salesperson engages earlier in the customer buying cycle. This early engagement gives them a chance to shape and influence the projects being considered. The salespeople also learn that selling a business case study provides the best qualification possible. They find out early whether the customer has real interest in a project. If the customer won't pay for a study, they're not serious about the project. So no-one wastes any more time on it.

Later, as the laggards in the sales team observe the success the early adopters enjoy, they will embrace customer success. But at the beginning the laggards won't be enthusiastic. So, it's best to concentrate on the sales team members who can immediately see the benefits. If possible, choose those who are the informal leaders, the influencers. Their success will carry greater weight.

The professional services teams will need to go through a similar transition. Again, Generation 3 vendors identify the informal leaders and have them show the way. The evolution begins with setting real and measurable objectives for all substantial projects. It's not necessary for small projects, particularly if they are of a technical nature.

Finally, the vendor will need to deal with partners. Again, some will be immediately enthusiastic, others more reserved. As far as possible, the vendors should work with the early adopters and let the others follow in time.

Quick Wins

As with any change management approach, it helps to identify and secure quick wins. These will vary by vendor. The vendor could trial a marketing campaign using a success outcome as the key message. They could prosecute a sales deal using the vendor's ability to enable a success outcome. They could run a small installed base campaign highlighting the value available from improving a success outcome. In Services, the teams can begin to set objectives for improvement of the success outcome from projects. Support (or others) can begin capturing data about customers to identify sales opportunities.

These quick wins help reinforce the value to the vendor of the customer success program.

Segmentation

In Step 2, the vendor decided on the ideal customer lifecycle and its steps. Vendors can now divide customers into three groups:

1. Those likely to accept the ideal lifecycle
2. Those who may accept the ideal lifecycle
3. Those unlikely to accept the ideal lifecycle

Generation 3 vendors start with the first group.

Tailored Engagement

Each customer will have a different customer success journey. Generation 3 vendors understand and adapt. They're comfortable not having a one-size-fits-all engagement process. For the early adopters, they'll need to tailor their engagement. Later, as the vendor and customers gain experience, the vendor can move to a more standardised approach.

Proving the Lifecycle — References

Sales organisations need good references. To gain references, they'll need to convert customers to the new success program and show progress. Initially, early adopter customers will move without references. But for more conservative customers, selling is much easier with references. The vendor will need a clear plan for developing references for their customer success program.

Most vendors have customers willing to take a reference call or reference visit. They're often passive referees, acting only when requested to do so by the vendor. Generation 3 vendors know they've been successful when customers become proactive advocates.

Services Projects

Generation 3 vendors understand Services projects will change. First, each project (above a minimum size) will need a real and measurable outcome. The customer and the vendor agree the outcome. Both parties acknowledge the objective as a joint commitment, not a commitment from the vendor alone.

Project management will include checks on likely outcome achievement. The agenda for project meetings and steering committee meetings need to include this topic. Both parties commit to taking remedial action if the outcome looks threatened.

The project isn't closed when the software goes live. It's an important milestone, but not the end of the job. The customer and vendor agree timing and responsibility for measuring results. Once the measurement has taken place, a joint presentation to the sponsoring executives for the project should take place.

The initial emphasis should be on setting project objectives and adjusting meeting agendas. As projects progress, the parties can focus more on measurement.

Support

Support departments in Cloud technology vendors now behave in a different way. In the past, they provided a reactive service. If the customer had a problem, the customer would notify the support department who would then respond to fix the issue.

Cloud vendors have learned that waiting for the customer to notify them of a problem is too slow. They need to monitor performance, identify potential problems and rectify them immediately. They often do this before the customer knows they have a problem.

Customer success programs offer a new expansion to the role of Support. Through Cloud, they've learned the skills of monitoring technical environments. Their role in a customer success program is to also monitor the business environment. The customer and vendor will have agreed KPIs or success measures. Support can monitor and report on these KPIs or success measures.

In a Cloud environment, Support has visibility on all activity. They can identify other potential issues and provide alerts. Customer success programs provide a wonderful opportunity for Support departments to expand their role and importance.

New Business

Vendors find it easier to position Generation 3 in new business deals than with existing customers. The existing customers have preconceptions about the vendor based on the way they've engaged in the past. A new prospect doesn't have that history.

In the early stages of a customer success program, the vendor won't have Generation 3 references. While customer success programs remain relatively new, the new business prospects will forgive this. In time, customer success programs will become the norm. Vendors without a proven program including references won't have the same leeway as they would today.

New business prospects love the Generation 3 Customer Success program. They love the focus on their success. They love the Success Consultants they meet. It's a great story to tell. Generation 3 vendors really can sell the dream.

Organisation Structure

To achieve success with their customer success program, vendors change the way they behave. As part of this, they may make changes in the organisation.

Some vendors opt for minimalist change. Others restructure the organisation. Some now have VPs of customer success. Some VPs of customer success have responsibility only for sales to existing customers. Other VPs own all customer-facing activities, including sales, marketing, services and support.

Generation 3 vendors consider several factors. First, they know the worst thing they can do is give the sales account managers a new title and not change anything about the way they work. The account manager arrives at the customer with a new business card reading 'Customer Success Manager'. They explain how the vendor has implemented a new program to ensure the customer's success. And then proceed to behave the way they always have. It's worse than doing nothing.

Generation 3 vendors take the time to plan their to-be state. They follow Stephen R Covey's (Covey, 1988) advice of beginning with the end in mind. They know they can't achieve the to-be state immediately. They're aware they need a staged implementation. But they have a clear picture of the destination. This helps them make sensible decisions as they begin the journey to an effective customer success program.

Regardless of the organisation structure chosen, vendors will benefit from a cross-functional team that leads the evolution of their customer success program. All customer-facing departments need to be represented.

Generation 3 vendors know that customer success needs to become part of their DNA. They need to drive sales engagement by identifying opportunities for customer success. That's how they sell projects, which drive demand for products and services. Services need to work with the customer to enable the customer success. Support needs to monitor the ongoing achievement of customer success. Marketing needs to provide the messaging and positioning to support customer success. R&D needs to deliver products that enhance customer success. Finance needs to prepare for sales deals where revenue is linked to customer success. HR needs to ensure the vendor has the people skills to enable customer success. IT needs to adopt new systems to help the focus on customer success.

In short, customer success affects every part of the organisation that deals with customers. Generation 3 vendors develop a clear, practical plan to evolve from the current state to the desired to-be state.

Step 5 — Staged Rollout

The success of a vendor's program will increase with a change management plan.

Generation 3 vendors tell all staff they're launching a customer success program. But they don't ask everyone to participate at first.

Generation 3 vendors ask selected customers and partners to take part.

Change Management

In Step 5, the vendor implements the plans formulated in Step 4.

A Generation 3 program can begin simply. Over time, it becomes pervasive. All customer-facing departments evolve.

A change management program improves success. The table on the following page shows the major topics needed in a change management plan.

Topic	Key Questions to Answer
Need for change	Why is the change necessary or desirable?
Vision	What is the 'big idea' behind the change? What do we want to achieve? What is the To-Be state?
Strategy	How will the vision be achieved? What are the highest priorities?
Resources	How much will the change cost? Who will be working on the program? For how long? Will there be offsetting benefits?
Executive buy-in	Commitment from which managers/executives is required? What is the current status?
Scope	What functions and/or activities are included in this change? Are there areas specifically excluded?
Time frame	When will this change start and when will it be completed?
What will change?	Who will be affected by the change and how? Is there a change to the organisation structure? What changes to processes, systems, people skills or partners are required? Are any transition arrangements needed?
Risks and restraining forces	What could adversely affect success? For significant risks and restraints, what contingencies are there?
Consolidate wins/ Evaluate progress	When, how and by whom will regular evaluations during the change be made?
Anchor change	How will success of the program be measured? When and who will do this?

Fig 28: Change management framework

Launching the Customer Success Program to Staff

Management inform all staff about the plans for Generation 3 Customer Success. They emphasise they won't take a big-bang approach. A subset of staff, customers and partners will work on Generation 3 at first. In time, it will be rolled out to everyone.

Generation 3 vendors have learned the quality of success consulting has a major impact on the success of the program. If they don't have in-house skills, they recruit. They expect people in this role to be expensive relative to other consultants in the organisation. It's likely they'll be the most expensive consultants. This isn't a role on which to cut corners.

Some salespeople assigned to the initial rollout won't feel confident discussing the detail of success outcomes. They'll understand the high-level idea and be able to explain it. But they won't be Success Consultants. They'll want to bring an impressive and credible Success Consultant to meetings with customer executives. They want consultants whose advice the customer executives will welcome and follow.

The initial staff chosen should have influence inside the vendor's organisation. Once they're successful, they'll positively affect the attitudes and behaviour of those around them. They should feel special, which they are. And management should welcome their input on evolving the program.

Rollout to Partners

Partners need a similar approach. The vendor chooses partners who will commit time and resources to the Generation 3 program. As with staff, some partners will embrace the concepts while others will be more reserved. Once the initial partners show success, the others will follow.

Rollout to Customers

The vendor identifies customers selected for initial rollout. The sales team discusses the proposed Generation 3 program and its benefits with the customer. The early adopter customers should then collaborate with the vendor in developing and refining the program.

As success occurs with the early adopters, rollout to other customers can move ahead.

> **Generation 3 vendors use the lens of the success outcome to generate innovative growth ideas.**
>
> ---
>
> There are four types of growth considered—Baseline, Extension, New-market and Disruptive.

Part 6 of the book covers Growth Planning in detail. The following provides a high-level overview of the growth categories.

Growth Category 1 — Baseline Growth

Most vendors want to sell more of their existing products. Defining a success outcome provides a new perspective on the vendor's products and services. Do the products and services enable the success outcome? It's possible some features are missing, in which case the vendor will need to plug the gaps. It's also possible there are features or elements which aren't important to the success outcome. Removing unnecessary features may simplify implementation and reduce costs.

The lens of a success outcome also assists ongoing decisions about improvements in core products. Generation 3 vendors give priority to new features that best enable or improve the success outcome.

Success outcomes drive increased sales for existing products and services.

Growth Category Two — Extension Growth

Baseline Growth focuses on increasing sales of existing products and services. Extension Growth identifies new products and services the vendor might offer. There are four types of extension growth— bridging the outcome gap, end-consumer outcomes, higher-level outcomes and secondary outcomes.

Bridging the Outcome Gap

The vendor's current products and services help enable a success outcome. But the vendor doesn't do everything required. Growth can occur by doing more of what the customer needs to achieve their success outcome.

End Consumer Outcomes

The technology vendor enables their customer's outcome. The relationship is almost always a B2B relationship. The vendor and their customer form part of a supply chain. The supply chain eventually serves end consumers. The vendor can generate ideas for new products and services by considering the outcome the end consumers want to achieve.

Higher Level Success Outcome

Success outcomes nest together. The highest success outcome (financial results) has smaller success outcomes that contribute. And these might have smaller success outcomes. Vendors apply the significance squared test. They choose a success outcome for which they are the most significant external supplier. But this success outcome is a subset of a bigger success outcome. The vendor doesn't focus on that bigger outcome as they don't pass the significance squared test—they aren't the most significant external vendor. They can grow by adding new products and services to become the most significant vendor for that bigger success outcome.

Secondary Success Outcomes

It's possible for a vendor to serve more than one success outcome. They have a primary success outcome. This may overlap with another, secondary outcome. The vendor can increase sales by offering more products and services for the secondary outcome.

Growth Category 3 — New-market Growth

For most vendors, it's tough to break into a new market. If the new market is a new geography, it's easiest for vendors to set up in locations where their customers already have operations.

Breaking into new industries is much tougher. A lack of reference accounts in a new industry often proves the biggest challenge. It's hard to win customers in a new industry without references in that industry. And without customers you can't have references.

Generation 3 Customer Success provides a new way to overcome this challenge. The vendor serves a success outcome in one industry.

136

They look for other industries with a similar success outcome. Instead of industry references, they use outcome references. The vendor shows prospects how they enable the success outcome in the other industry.

Growth Category 4 — Disruptive Growth

Most vendors would love to grow by disrupting the market they serve. We see more and more disruptive products and services, some producing spectacular results for the disruptor. Generation 3 offers three types of disruptive growth planning—New Delivery, Add-on Outcome and New Outcome.

PART 6
GENERATION 3 GROWTH PLANNING

> **Success Outcomes provide a new lens through which to consider growth.**
>
> ---
>
> Generation 3 vendors conduct a regular cycle of growth planning using this lens.
>
> Generation 3 vendors consider four categories of growth—Baseline, Extension, New-market and Disruptive.
>
> After generating lots of ideas, they use Capability Circles to choose those with which to proceed.

Geoffrey Moore introduced the technology sector to the Technology Adoption Life-Cycle (Moore, 1991). He documented the stages every product or service goes through and how growth varies at each stage. It's slow during the early adopter phase, speeds up during the early majority, then slows and declines in the late majority and laggard phases. Vendors with products in the early majority phase don't have a problem with growth. For everyone else, growth presents a challenge.

Generation 3 vendors understand this lifecycle applies to them. So, they constantly plan for new sources of growth. And they use a new lens to plan that growth—the success outcome they serve.

Generation 3 growth planning uses four different types of growth—Baseline, Extension, New-market and Disruptive. They form a somewhat fortuitous acronym—BEND. It's fortuitous as vendors need a flexible growth planning framework. The industry changes quickly. Vendors need a growth planning process that can adapt or bend to suit the changing environment.

Generating Growth Ideas

Smart, competent people lead most technology vendors. These leaders don't find it difficult to generate growth ideas. Often, the challenge isn't in generating ideas, but in choosing which ones to pursue.

Generation 3 Growth offers a few advantages as a growth planning approach. First, it provides a simple context for idea generation—the success outcome. The success outcome helps align everyone's thinking around how to increase revenue by better serving the customer.

Second, Generation 3 Growth provides a step-by-step method for generating ideas. Everyone can follow the process, and it helps everyone stay focused.

Third, it offers a method for prioritising and choosing the ideas to pursue. Capability Circles helps everyone understand why some ideas move forward, while others don't.

Finally, Generation 3 Growth helps generate a practical plan of action.

Let's illustrate how success outcomes can help generate growth ideas with two examples from outside the technology industry. We'll start with an historical example—camera film manufacturers. What success outcome did the camera film business serve? The obvious answer might be taking photos. But consider why people take photos. The word memories might come to mind. Film manufacturers were in the business of preserving memories.

But people also liked to show other people the printed photos. In some cases, they would send copies of prints to family or friends. They wanted to share the memories. The outcome was broader—to preserve and share memories. The to-be state for camera film customers was memories preserved and shared.

How could camera film manufacturers of the past have used this knowledge of the outcome they served? They could have explored all the ways to preserve and share memories. Digital photography was possible. How about online photo storage to preserve memories? Take this one step further and use online storage to share those memories. What about tools to improve the quality of the images? Perhaps camera film manufacturers could have developed tools like Photoshop. Those innovations all exist today. But, a camera film manufacturer that understood the success outcome could have pioneered the innovations. Their business would have flourished.

Let's consider a different example—sports car manufacturers. What is the success outcome that sports car manufacturers serve? The thrill of driving fast? Consider the limited opportunity to use the true capability of a sports car in everyday driving. That's probably not the answer.

Think about people who own sports cars. They typically have one thing in common—they enjoy being noticed. Perhaps the success outcome served by sports car manufacturers is the owners being noticed. The sports car manufacturers' outcome is 'customer noticed'. The to-be state for sports car owners is 'noticed'.

Perhaps this definition could be refined for different sports cars and their success outcomes. For Ferrari, perhaps its 'customers noticed, success and style'. Lamborghini might be 'customers noticed, and out there'. For McLaren, perhaps its 'customers noticed, racing enthusiast'.

Let's consider the Ferrari success outcome. What other products or services could Ferrari offer that would fit 'customers noticed, success and style'? Motor yachts might fit. Ferrari already offers watches and clothing bearing the Ferrari brand. Go one step further. Perhaps Ferrari could offer residences—apartment buildings that conveyed the 'success and style' message.

Sports car manufacturers might help their customers be noticed in some other way. Perhaps they could place an announcement in a local newspaper or on social media when someone bought one of their cars. The customer would certainly feel noticed.

These examples illustrate the Generation 3 approach. First, define the success outcome. Then, use the success outcome to generate growth ideas.

Choosing the Success Outcome

As we've discussed, choosing the success outcome a vendor serves offers considerable latitude. It's not an exact science. Vendors may choose differently depending on factors such as:

- the strategic direction the vendor wants to take
- the reaction of customers
- the potential for growth

Vendors in the same industry and with comparable products may choose different success outcomes to serve. One vendor may plan to expand the range of products it offers. Another may choose to deepen their expertise in a narrow area of key importance to customers. These vendors would not choose the same success outcome. Generation 3 Customer Success offers a new opportunity for vendors to differentiate.

With a success outcome chosen, Generation 3 vendors use Generation 3 Growth to create growth ideas. The program offers four categories of growth—baseline, extension, new-market and disruptive. But first, it's worth considering retention of existing revenue.

The First Step in Growth is to Retain Existing Revenue

It's hard to grow if the existing base of revenue isn't stable. Subscription pricing has made that base far less stable. Loss of revenue can take two forms. First, the customer can switch vendors. Because licence fees aren't paid upfront anymore, it's financially easier to switch vendors. Of course, that's not the only consideration. If the customer switched vendors, they would still face the disruption of implementing another product. But the customer may decide the lack of success with the first vendor makes a change inevitable. Also, the customers may be angry and want to punish the first vendor. It's easier for them to do so.

The second loss of revenue comes from lower than expected usage. In the days of perpetual licences, the customer bought the licences needed upfront. The vendor might offer additional discounts to also include future users in the initial bundle. This practice created licences that sat on the shelf—shelfware.

When customers buy subscriptions, they typically pay only for the number of users needed immediately. If they don't achieve success, usage will not increase and may even decline. Even if the customer doesn't switch vendors, the vendor's revenue will be much lower than expected.

Through a customer success program, vendors aim to protect existing revenue and then increase usage for additional revenue. They want churn to be as low as possible. An effective customer success program provides the best way to minimise churn and increase usage.

Growth Categories

Let's now consider the Generation 3 Growth Categories.

Growth Category 1 — Baseline Growth

Vendors want to sell more of their existing products. Choosing a success outcome provides a new perspective on the features and functions needed in the vendor's products and services. Do the products and services enable the success outcome they've chosen?

It's possible they've missed some important features, in which case they'll need to plug those gaps. It's also possible some features of their current offering aren't important to enabling the success outcome. Removing unnecessary features may simplify implementation and reduce costs.

Using the lens of a success outcome also assists in making decisions about improvements in core products. They'll prioritise new features that best enable or improve the success outcome.

The following diagram illustrates the concept. The vendor had a set of products and services (on the left). When they added the perspective of the success outcome, they realised the shape of their products and services needed to change. They could drop some products and services and add others. They ended up with a set of products and services well-shaped for the success outcome they'd chosen.

Fig 29: Products and services must fit the success outcome

Selling the Success Outcome

Baseline Growth isn't only about ensuring the vendor's products and services fit the success outcome. The success outcome can generate demand for existing products and services. We can again learn from *The Challenger Customer* (Adamson, 2015). Generation 3 vendors want to provide Commercial Insight to their customers. The success outcome provides a vehicle for doing so.

The success outcome describes a to-be state the customer can achieve. But many customers won't have looked at their business in that way. For example:

- not all ERP customers will realise the task is to enable 'effective operations'
- not all marketing automation customers will understand they must ensure sufficient pipeline to allow sales to reach their targets
- not all content management customers will think the task is to ensure 'informed and governed decisions'

Introducing success outcomes to a customer can help them see their business in a new light. To use Challenger thinking, a success outcome can provide new Commercial Insight. The Generation 3 vendor can then help them develop a plan to achieve the success outcome. That planning process will generate new projects from which the vendor can derive revenue. Everyone wins.

Growth Category Two — Extension Growth

Baseline Growth helps increase sales of existing products and services. Extension Growth helps identify new products and services the vendor might offer. There are four types of extension growth—bridging the outcome gap, end-consumer outcome, higher-level outcomes and secondary outcomes.

Bridging the Outcome Gap

The vendor's current products and services help enable a success outcome. But the vendor doesn't do everything required.

Fig 30: There's a gap between product and success outcomes

The outer circle represents all the products, services and activities needed by the customer to achieve the success outcome. The inner circle represents the products and services the vendor provides. Other suppliers also provide products and services. And the customer carries out activities themselves.

The vendor can grow by doing more of what the customer needs to achieve the success outcome.

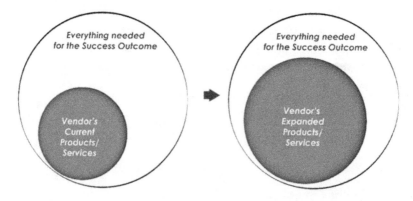

Fig 31: Grow by providing more of the success outcome

To generate ideas for new products or services, Generation 3 vendors list everything the customer needs to achieve the success outcome. They tick everything they currently provide. The difference between what the customer needs and what the vendor provides is the outcome gap. The vendor can grow by bridging the outcome gap. This will involve displacing other vendors or taking over activities currently performed by the customer. The total needs of the customer remain unchanged, but the vendor provides a greater share.

End-Consumers' Outcomes

Generation 3 vendors enable their customers' success outcome. In turn, the vendor's customers have their own customers. At the end of the supply chain, there are end-consumers. The vendor can generate ideas for new products and services by considering the success outcome the end-consumers want to achieve.

To illustrate, imagine a family restaurant. Families who come to the restaurant want to have fun as well as eat. Let's say their success outcome is 'fun family meal'.

Now consider a food manufacturer—let's say they make chicken nuggets. Could the manufacturer make chicken nuggets that help the families achieve their success outcome of 'fun family meal'? What about nuggets in funny animal shapes? Or have a small number of nuggets with a special shape, and any kid who gets a nugget in that shape gets a prize? Perhaps they could have different-coloured nuggets. Or nuggets that make a funny noise when a kid bites one (parents will hate that, but the kids would love it).

The food manufacturer then approaches the owner of the family restaurant. They show how their new nuggets will help the restaurant deliver the success outcome of 'fun family meal'. The owner agrees and buys the nuggets. The restaurant and the food manufacturer both win.

Higher Level Success Outcome

Serving a higher-level success outcome presents another way to sell new products and services. Let's step through the approach.

The vendor serves a success outcome for which they are significant.

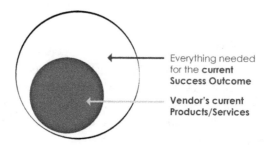

Fig 32: Vendor's current success outcome

This success outcome will be a subset of a bigger success outcome the customer wants to achieve.

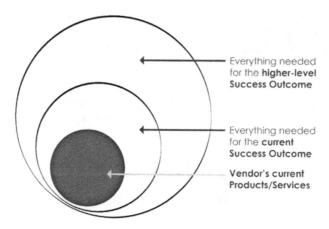

Fig 33: Current outcome and higher-level outcome

The vendor can grow by offering products and services that enable the higher-level outcome, i.e. the outer circle.

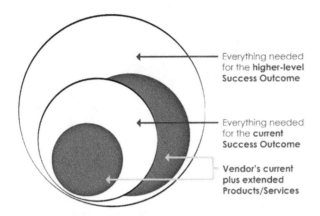

Everything needed for the **higher-level** Success Outcome

Everything needed for the **current** Success Outcome

Vendor's current plus extended Products/Services

Fig 34: Provide more for the higher-level outcome

To illustrate, imagine the vendor provides a content management package. Managers in the customer use information from the content management system to inform their decisions. The success outcome served by the vendor might be 'informed decisions'.

The customer may need decisions to be made following a protocol (very common in government). They need to be able to check the protocol was followed—they need to govern the decision-making process. A higher-level outcome for the customer might be 'informed and governed decisions'. The vendor might acquire a product that helps manage the process. Now they offer both content management software and decision-making software. This allows the vendor to enable the higher-level outcome of 'informed and governed decisions'.

Secondary Success Outcomes

It's possible for a vendor to serve more than one success outcome. There's a primary success outcome. But this may overlap with another, secondary outcome. The vendor can increase sales by offering more products and services for the secondary outcome. Let's step through the approach.

The vendor serves a success outcome:

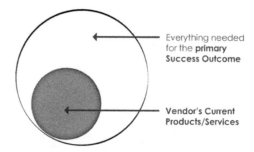

Fig 35: The vendor's current success outcome

But the vendor's current products and services also serve a secondary success outcome.

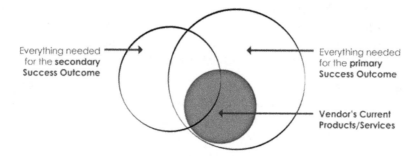

Fig 36: The vendor serves a secondary outcome

The vendor can grow by extending their range of products and services into the secondary outcome, i.e. to do more to help the customer achieve this secondary success outcome:

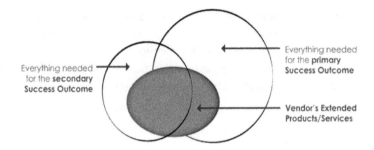

Fig 37: Provide more for the secondary outcome

To illustrate, imagine a CRM vendor. The CRM vendor helps sales teams become disciplined. The customer wants their sales teams to:

- follow a disciplined sales process
- record details of customer interactions
- store proposals and quotations
- keep the status of any opportunity up-to-date

The primary outcome for the customer is 'disciplined sales team'.

The customer also uses the CRM package to do a small amount of lead generation activity. The secondary outcome might be 'leads generated'. To grow, the vendor could acquire a marketing automation product. The customer would see a natural synergy, the vendor would increase sales revenue and develop a deeper bond with the customer.

Growth Category 3 — New-market Growth

For most vendors, it's tough to break into a new market. If the new market is a new geography, it's easiest for vendors to set up in locations where their customers have operations. The vendor can then use these customers as the foundation from which to spread to other businesses in the new geography.

Breaking into new industries can be much tougher. Deciding which industries to target requires careful consideration. A lack of reference accounts in a new industry often proves the biggest challenge. It's hard to win customers in a new industry without references in that industry. And without customers in the industry you don't have references.

Generation 3 Customer Success provides a new way to overcome this challenge. The vendor serves a success outcome in one industry. They look for other industries with a similar success outcome. Instead of industry references, they use outcome references. The vendor shows prospects how they enable the success outcome in the other industry.

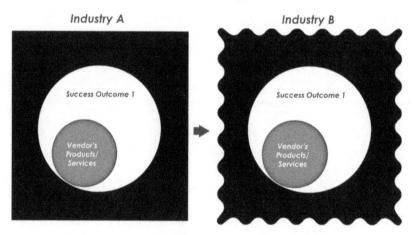

Fig 38: Same success outcome, different industry

To illustrate, imagine a marketing automation vendor with a specialty niche in commercial banking. The banks want to engage with key executives in corporate prospects. They use a marketing automation tool to drive campaigns and nurture relationships. The success outcome for the banks might be 'prospect executives nurtured'.

The vendor has decided they want to grow revenue by breaking into a new industry. Using Generation 3 thinking, they look for industries with a similar success outcome to banking. They identify insurance as a possibility. The insurance companies want the business from large corporations. They need to drive campaigns and nurture relationships with key executives. Their success outcome turns out to be the same as the banks'—'prospect executives nurtured'.

The vendor shows the corporate insurance market how they can nurture prospect executives. The vendor breaks into the insurance industry, despite not having references in that industry.

Generation 3 thinking has helped the vendor identify a viable market to target. And given them the ability to break into that industry.

Growth Category 4 — Disruptive Growth

Most vendors like the idea of growing by disrupting their competitors. In technology, we see more and more disruptive products and services, some producing spectacular results for the disruptor. In this chapter, we'll show how Generation 3 thinking can help generate ideas for disruptive growth.

But disruption can also have a negative aspect. A vendor can fall victim to disruption. We'll deal in a later section with how Generation 3 thinking can help a vendor guard against negative disruption.

Lots of different external factors can result in disruption of an industry. Regulatory changes, economic changes, wars, terrorism, and much more can disrupt an industry. In the technology world, the most common disruptor is technology itself. In the creation of positive disruption for a vendor, technology will be the most common tool used.

Technological Disruptors

The following examples of technological disruptors can all be used to generate ideas for new products and services.

Artificial Intelligence

Artificial Intelligence has promised much, but the rate of improvement until recently has been slower than many hoped. In more recent times, the rate of change has increased. Few now doubt that AI will have a significant impact on everyone's daily lives. Some people have concerns about the singularity—the point at which machines can improve themselves more effectively than humans can improve them.

Regardless, AI has the potential to create substantial disruption in the technology sector.

Robotics

We see considerable speculation about the impact of robotics on existing jobs. Many people worry their jobs will disappear. Some industries such as aged care will face major change. Technology vendors supporting industries most affected by robotics have a great opportunity. They can adapt their products and services to robotics and disrupt competitors.

Big Data

Big data has already had a significant influence on the technology sector and its customers. The ability to collate, process and make sense of massive quantities of data provides great insights. This trend will continue.

Internet of Things

The Internet of things will continue to disrupt traditional industries and offers significant opportunities for technology vendors.

Cloud

The whole technology industry is moving to the Cloud. As true utility-based computing becomes pervasive, Cloud will further impact our industry.

Online Collaboration

The growing number of tools facilitating online collaboration is changing basic work patterns within organisations. Increasingly, these tools will also change the interaction between organisations.

Blockchain

Many commentators predict blockchain will have as much impact as the internet in re-shaping our lives. There's massive investment in this technology happening around the world.

All the above disruptors can help technology vendors create new products and services and grow their business. Let's now consider the three types of Disruptive Growth.

New Delivery Approach

New Delivery involves finding new ways to deliver an existing success outcome. It looks like this:

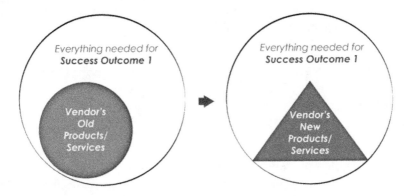

Fig 39: Deliver same success outcome in different way

To illustrate, consider the Sony Walkman, launched in 1979. Sony initially offered a cassette tape version which evolved to a portable CD player. The Walkman reigned supreme for years. The success outcome served by the Walkman might be 'music made portable'. Then, in 1987, a Korean company introduced the first MP3 player. The success outcome of 'music made portable' remained unchanged, but the delivery changed. MP3 players and their successors disrupted and finally killed the market for the traditional Walkman.

Netflix provides a more recent example. They disrupted the video-store industry. The video-stores' success outcome might have been 'entertained at home'. The first disruption by Netflix overcame the need to go to a store to rent a video. Netflix customers could order online, and Netflix would deliver. They enabled the same success outcome of 'entertained at home' but used a new delivery method. Netflix then went a step further and provided video streaming. And that really was the death-knell for video stores (and Netflix's own video business, by the way). Again, the same success outcome but a new delivery method.

In the past, searching for new delivery methods involved analysing customers' problems and solving them in new ways. It's a logical approach but has an important downside. We discussed current-solution blindness in an earlier section. When a group starts their thinking with a current problem, they'll be aware there's a current solution. The natural tendency is to tweak the current solution, to take the path of least resistance. Why bother trying to create something new and innovative if tweaks to an existing solution will do the job? It's difficult to break away from the current solutions when the frame of reference is the current problem.

Generation 3 vendors don't start with the current problems. They focus on the success outcome or to-be state. This breaks the tie to the current solutions. It offers an opportunity to generate innovative and different ideas.

Once they've come up with ideas, Generation 3 vendors verify those ideas enable the success outcome. Now they consider the customer's current problems. They check the new delivery method solves the existing problems. Significant problems can disappear with an innovative new delivery approach. If the previous problems remain unsolved and significant, the vendor can revisit the new delivery method.

Add-on Outcome

Creating an add-on outcome involves taking an existing success outcome and adding a new and innovative element to it:

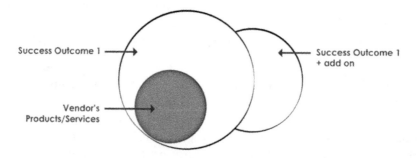

Fig 40: Add to an existing success outcome

The vendor provides new products and services that enable the current outcome plus the add-on. Note that the new products and services may be completely different from those offered to enable the previous success outcome:

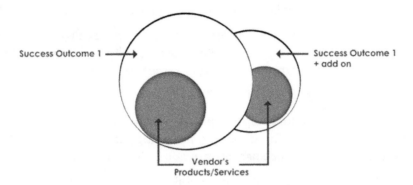

Fig 41: Add products/services for the add-on outcome

To illustrate, let's consider personal productivity and companies that once thrived but then plummeted. In the past, business people used paper-based daily planners. These were often leather folders. They contained pages for contacts, calendars, to-do lists and information such as public holidays, etc. The manufacturers of daily planners also provided training courses in personal productivity. They thrived. The success outcome of a daily planner company might be 'business information captured'.

But if someone lost their daily planner, they lost everything. It was a nightmare. And then the PalmPilot came along. It put all this business information on a handheld device and backed the information up. Palm added a new success outcome—'business information captured and backed-up'. It was a breakthrough and Palm took off as a company. Mobile phones later appeared with the same offering and Palm matched them with a phone of their own.

Some years later, BlackBerry added push email on the mobile device. They changed the success outcome for mobile devices to something like 'business connected'. Another breakthrough and BlackBerry took off.

Then the iPhone came along. The iPhone added personal apps, social media, music. Apple had added something further to the success outcome. Their success outcome became 'personal and business connected'. iPhone sales went crazy. Android followed a year later.

These are all examples of add-on outcomes. A company took an existing success outcome, added a new element and created a new outcome. And in so doing, disrupted all other competitors.

There's a lesson from this history of personal productivity tools. If there's an entrenched vendor with strong loyalty, the best way to dislodge them is to create a different success outcome.

New Success Outcome

The third approach to disruptive growth involves creating an entirely new success outcome. The disruptive technology discussed earlier can help create success outcomes not previously imagined.

Driverless cars, voice control of mobile devices (e.g. Siri), remote access and control of heating or cooling in a house, and fridges and cupboards that automatically replenish contents all provide examples of technology creating new success outcomes.

Generation 3 vendors monitor these and other technological disruptors. They consider whether these disruptors can create new success outcomes they can serve. They know that if they can make a breakthrough in creating a new success outcome and then enable that outcome, their revenue can explode.

Generation 3 vendors plan for growth regularly. They create lots of innovative ideas. They'll almost always have too many to implement them all. Their next step is to sort and prioritise the ideas then generate a practical action plan.

Core Capabilities

In choosing ideas to progress, Generation 3 vendors first consider proximity to the vendor's core capabilities. Core capabilities are the things the vendor does consistently well. A new idea will be easier to implement if it's close to core capabilities. The vendor is likely to have much of the skill needed. And customers are more likely to accept the new product or service if it's close to the vendor's core capabilities.

When considering core capabilities, Generation 3 vendors usually identify many capabilities. They need to prioritise. Again, the success outcome can help. They prioritise capabilities that directly contribute to enabling the success outcome.

A list of capabilities directly contributing to the success outcome could still be a lengthy list. If this occurs, a second filter can assist. The vendor focuses on capabilities the customer considers important when choosing suppliers. They drop capabilities that aren't key to the customers' choice of suppliers.

Capability Circles

Capability circles provide a simple vehicle to visualise the ranking of ideas. Generation 3 vendors place core capabilities in circle one, the centre circle.

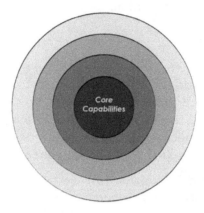

Fig 42: Rank growth ideas using capability circles

The vendor rates each idea on proximity to core capabilities. To visualise this proximity, they place each idea in a circle. Ideas close to core capabilities go in circle two, the first ring out from the centre. Ideas further away go in circle three and ideas furthest from core capabilities go in circle four. This provides the first cut prioritisation of ideas.

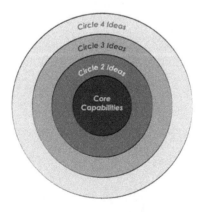

Fig 43: Add additional criteria to ranking

However, rating ideas solely on proximity to core capabilities isn't enough. A second step takes account of other factors such as:

- cost
- potential revenue
- ease of implementation
- return on investment
- cultural fit
- the competitors for a new product or service

Each vendor will decide these secondary factors themselves. To keep things practical, they choose the three most important factors. Combined with proximity to core capabilities, this provides enough prioritisation.

The cycle assigned to each idea may change based on these secondary factors. For example, an idea close to core capabilities would sit in circle two. But if that idea has low scores on the other factors, it may move to circle three or circle four.

On the other hand, an idea in circle three on proximity but with high ratings on the other factors might move into circle two.

The circles will show priority and timing. The vendor will implement ideas in circle two, probably in the current year or next year.

The vendor is likely to implement ideas in circle three but commencing in one to two years' time. Ideas in circle four need further analysis before the vendor decides whether to proceed.

A Practical Action Plan

Once the vendor has prioritised the ideas, they need an action plan. The ideas will all sound appealing. The temptation to launch many of them will be difficult to resist. Most organisations have experience of over-ambitious plans.

Adept Generation 3 vendors appraise the resources they can apply to development of new products and services. They make sensible decisions about a limited number of projects they can sustain. And then they execute.

PART 7
GENERATION 3 MARKETING

> **Generation 3 vendors use the success outcome they enable as the central theme of their marketing.**
>
> ---
>
> Success outcomes:
>
> - help define mission, vision, identity, competitive differentiation, segmentation
>
> - drive lead generation
>
> - help protect against disruption

Generation 3 thinking offers wonderful opportunities for marketing. Everything can change. It offers the chance to be different from and better than all competitors.

What Business Is the Vendor in?

When someone asks a vendor what they do, most respond with a description of their products or services. They'll say things like 'We're an ERP software company' or 'We're a Cloud services provider'.

But customers and prospects don't care about a vendor's products. They only care about the outcomes they want to achieve. When a vendor describes themselves based on their own products and services, they don't create any rapport or empathy. The customer or prospect will lose interest and switch off.

Generation 3 vendors describe themselves differently. The Generation 3 ERP vendor might say 'We make operations more effective'. Think about a harried Chief Operating Officer who needs to improve the effectiveness of their operations. Which phrase is likely to get their attention—ERP software company or an enabler of effective operations?

Similarly, the marketing automation vendor might say 'We're a pipeline-creation company'. VPs of Marketing, under pressure to deliver leads the sales team can close, will find this term appealing.

If a vendor has clarity about the success outcome they deliver, what better way of defining their business could there be?

Mission Statement and Tagline

Lots of mission statements waffle. They contain long words and long sentences that convey little meaning. Mission statements should be clear, distinct and short. They should create a picture in the mind of the audience that gives clarity on what the vendor aims to do.

When defining a success outcome, Generation 3 vendors apply the significance squared test. They adopt a success outcome for which they are significant, and which is significant to the customer. The same test can apply to mission statements. Mission statements should focus on something to which the vendor significantly contributes, and something significant to the customer.

Many mission statements fail the first of these tests. The vendor does not contribute significantly to what's described in the mission statement. We often see 'boil the ocean' statements. They express aspirations so lofty the vendor has little chance of having any real impact. Statements such as 'Our products will green the planet' and 'Our services deliver financial well-being for all' come to mind.

Generation 3 vendors' taglines reflect their success outcomes. An ERP vendor might use 'effective operations enabled'. Or if they serve a particular niche such as Finance they could use 'effective operations for Finance'. The marketing automation vendor might use 'sales pipeline delivered' or 'qualified leads delivered'.

In both cases, the tagline resonates with the outcome the customer wants to achieve. Potential customers see the tagline and ask, 'How do you do that?'. If that happens, the tagline has served its purpose. It got the interest of a potential prospect.

Generation 3 vendors have mission statements and taglines that reflect the success outcome they serve.

Identity

In marketing circles, it's understood organisations need an identity—something for which they're known. And which sets them apart from competitors. Building an identity around a success outcome can deliver this differentiation. For example, the ERP vendor might be 'the world's best enabler of effective operations for Finance'. The marketing automation vendor might be 'the fastest to deliver sales pipeline'.

Identity drives messaging and competitive differentiation. Generation 3 vendors build their identity around the success outcome they serve.

Segmentation

The most common segmentation for a vendor's customers uses revenue potential. Customers with large revenue potential are A accounts or major accounts or strategic accounts. Smaller customers are B or C accounts. There's logic to this, as the 80/20 rule is alive and well. A small percentage of the customers provide most of the revenue. Vendors want to ensure they engage closely with the customers providing the most revenue. They manage customers with smaller revenue potential using some form of one-to-many structure.

But revenue potential does not determine the way the customer behaves or the way they'd like to engage with the vendor. Some large customers want the vendor to work closely with them. They value the vendor's help. Other large customers keep the vendor at arm's length, only engaging when they have no alternative. Smaller customers can display the same characteristics. Some value close engagement with the vendor, others prefer distance.

Generation 3 vendors understand this dichotomy. They know all customers want to achieve a success outcome, but each has a different way of getting there. Using the customer's preference on engagement model provides another method of segmentation. One segment might consist of all customers engaging using the ideal customer lifecycle. Another group of customers may not yet have embraced the ideal lifecycle, but they like parts of it. And they may be influenced to adopt the ideal lifecycle. Another group of customers may only want an arm's-length relationship.

Generation 3 vendors understand the customer's preferred engagement model. They use this as another criterion for segmentation.

Lead Generation

The segmentation used for existing customers can also apply to new business lead generation. Generation 3 vendors seek prospects who see the value of a focus on enabling a success outcome. Marketing campaigns can all focus on success outcomes.

Nurture

Engagement with customers and prospects is a long-term practice. Short bursts of activity followed by gaps with little contact don't work, either with customers or prospects.

Generation 3 vendors build a nurture program. Content marketing plays a significant role. The content marketing is not about the vendor's products or services. It's about the success outcome. The vendor publishes insights into how to achieve or improve success outcomes. They build their identity around this model.

When it's time for customers or prospects to buy, the vendor has positioned themselves as a success outcome expert. They're far more likely to win the business.

Insights from the Long-term Sales Funnel

We discussed earlier how the joint planning process with customers provides insight into topics the customers care about. Marketing can use this data to identify trends and predict the need for future products and services.

They can also use the information to position themselves as market leaders when a new trend emerges.

Future-proofing

Technology vendors are particularly susceptible to disruptive change. Technology is changing faster and faster. As a result, vendors can be made obsolete much faster than ever before.

Some vendors centre their identity and mission around their products and services. This exposes them to technological disruption. Their current products or services can quickly be made obsolete. The examples of BlackBerry making Palm Pilots obsolete, then Apple superseding BlackBerry reinforce how quickly technology companies can succumb.

Generation 3 vendors centre their identity and mission around the success outcome they serve. This keeps them open to new and better ways to deliver the success outcome. If a disruptive technology comes along, they're more likely to invest in it. They will see it as an opportunity rather than a threat—they will see a better way to deliver the success outcome. And they can adopt the new technology without changing their business focus.

Protecting the Business

Collateral Damage

Generation 3 vendors know customers only care about the success outcome. They don't care about the vendor's products or services. The vendor's products are a means to an end, not an end in themselves.

If the customer does not achieve their success outcome, they'll make changes. The executives are like the coach of a sports team on a losing run. The coach will drop some players. The coach needs to act. Business is the same. If they don't achieve the success outcome, the executives need to act. It's easy to blame a vendor. Replacing the vendor is a decisive action and buys the executives time. The vendor may not have been at fault, but the customer drops them anyway. We call this collateral damage.

Generation 3 vendors minimise the risk of becoming collateral damage. They appreciate all the things the customer must do to achieve the success outcome. And they help with as much as possible. They don't leave things to chance. They help the customer get everything needed for customer success right.

Less Open to Competitive Threat

Competitors claim their products are superior or cheaper or both. The technology industry is a tough competitive market. Vendors always face the threat of replacement.

If a vendor adds additional value through enabling the whole success outcome, customers are less likely to drop them. Competitors would need large differences in features or price to have any chance.

Disruption

Disruptors provide a very effective way for a vendor to grow. But those same disruptors can present a threat. A competitor can adopt a new technology or create a new success outcome and disrupt an existing vendor.

Generation 3 vendors look for threats using the same structure as for planning growth. They look for organisations creating a new way to deliver the vendor's existing success outcome. They look for organisations creating an add-on outcome. And they look for organisations working on completely new success outcomes.

They don't limit their search to existing competitors. They understand disruption can bring different organisations into their marketplace. They're aware of developments in artificial intelligence, robotics, big data, Cloud, Internet of things, online collaboration and blockchain. And they have a process for researching and reviewing the potential disruptors to their business.

CONCLUSION

In Part 1, we examined the explosion of interest in customer success programs. Subscription pricing has shifted power back to the customers. If customers aren't successful, they can more easily switch vendors. Even if they don't switch, the vendor doesn't get the growth they'd hoped for. And may even see a decline in revenue from a customer. There's now a much greater financial imperative to ensure customers are successful.

We next explored the three generations of engagement. Generation 1 vendors (Features Generation) respond to the customers' requirements. Generation 2 vendors (Solution Generation) solve the customer's current problems. Generation 3 vendors (Outcome Generation) enable future results through a new to-be state. We discussed how Generation 2 has served the technology industry well for over a quarter of a century. But the increased pace of change in business requires it to evolve. It's too slow trying to solve current problems. By the time that happens, new ones have arrived. Generation 3 is more forward-looking. It focuses on a future to-be state and takes account of anticipated change.

Part 1 of the book concluded by introducing success outcomes. We looked at the difference between product outcomes (the direct benefit from products and services) and success outcomes (the broader outcome the customer really wants to achieve). We

173

reinforced the idea that customers don't care about a vendor's products and services—they only care about the outcome they want to achieve.

For this reason, Generation 3 vendors moved past a focus on products and product outcomes. They help their customers achieve the success outcome the customers care about.

In Part 2, we examined the Generation 3 Customer Success program. We introduced DEEP Engagement—the lifecycle for ideal customers. We looked at the four phases—Develop, Evaluate, Execute and Prosper and some examples of the steps in an ideal customer lifecycle. We noted that not all customers would become ideal customers and the need for engagement models for this non-ideal group.

We then considered the key principles that underscore DEEP Engagement, looked at success consulting and then moved on to measurement. Under the latter, we examined entry-level measures, product outcome measures, success outcome measures and project outcome measures.

Part 3 focused on new business sales—sales to organisations with whom the vendor has no prior relationship. We explored how Generation 3 vendors 'sell the dream'—the success outcome they serve.

In Part 4, we introduced a theory of customer loyalty. Loyalty has two elements—what's provided (the percentage of the success outcome) and how it's delivered (the customer experience). We then added the potential for extraordinary loyalty through a new and much-loved success outcome.

In Part 5, we examined the six steps to implement a Generation 3 Customer Success program:

- Define the success outcome
- Define the to-be state
- Analyse execution capability
- Develop an implementation plan
- Staged rollout
- Growth planning

In Part 6 we explored Growth Planning in more detail. We looked at four different types of growth:

- Baseline
- Extension
- New-market
- Disruptive

We noted Generation 3 vendors produce lots of ideas. They then use Capability Circles to create a practical list of ideas and an action plan.

Finally, in Part 7, we considered the impact of Generation 3 on Marketing.

END WORDS

There's a sense of inevitability to the move to the Outcome Generation and the related uptake of customer success programs. The field gains momentum by the day. But it's still young as a discipline. And the way vendors engage with customers will always vary. Each vendor will have ideas on the best way to develop relationships and trust and ultimately to grow loyal revenue.

Customer Success feels a lot like Customer Relationship Management felt in the late '90s and early 2000s. Vendors were paying attention. Some jumped in, others waited. But all had interest. In time, every vendor would have a customer relationship management program. CRM software emerged, dominated at first by Siebel. And then disrupted and dominated by Salesforce.

There's a sense that customer success is following the same pattern. And that it will also become as pervasive.

Most of what's described in the Generation 3 Customer Success program is already in use. Most vendors already do some elements. They've already moved past Generation 2 in some areas.

The journey to Generation 3 for some won't be a long one—they don't have far to go. For others, it may take a little longer. The aim is to unify all elements of a vendor's business around a single theme—serving the customer's success outcome. It gives everyone in the business a common grounding and focus.

The program draws on over five years of developing and running a customer success program (although we didn't know to call it that, at the time) based around outcomes. We learned hard lessons along the way.

Now, there is a cadre of smart, competent people writing books and articles from which we can learn. Those five years of experience and reading other people's insights have come together in this book.

Ultimately, the book has a single purpose. To enable vendors to achieve the success outcome of Loyal Revenue Growth. I sincerely hope it proves of value to you.

Next Steps

You can learn more about Generation 3 Customer Success at our website: www.gen3cs.com. You'll find information and tools.

If you're interested in the Generation 3 Customer Success program but aren't yet ready to commit, we offer an interim step. We'll conduct a customer success study. We'll run some education and then carry out some of the first steps in the program. You'll get a report that provides everything you need to decide if the program is right for you. And even if you don't proceed, you'll have valuable take-aways you can use immediately.

If you decide to move forward, we'll run the full program. It's a series of planning meetings. We'll use our framework to help you develop a customer success program tailored to your business. And you'll have a practical, achievable implementation plan.

Acknowledgements

This book has been through two significant iterations. I first wrote it as a work of business fiction. Tanya Graham, Nick Maley, Glenn Wright, Will Bosma, Mark Pretty and Carter Lloyds were all kind enough to read various drafts. All identified opportunities for improvement and were good enough to share their insights. All had multiple rounds of input.

Terry Onica, a global automotive expert, provided input on that first iteration. Daniel Lender also added his valuable insights.

As part of gaining feedback, I first presented the book's concepts in PowerPoint. My thanks to David Johnson, Michael Price, Stim Robinson, Charles Summers, Anton Chilton (with Carter Lloyds), Paul Rush and Sujoy Roychaudhury. I used their input to create the first draft of the manuscript.

The manuscript was then handed to Red Raven Books for editing. Editor James Roberts guided my attention to problems with style and structure and then helped me correct those deficiencies.

Around this time, I began a program by Dent Global called Key Person of Influence (KPI). One of the pillars of the course is the Publish section. Amongst other assistance, the program helps course attendees write a book. I thought this part of the course would be a breeze, as I'd already written my book. I submitted a synopsis to the Publish mentor, seeking feedback on my book for final polishing. The very knowledgeable and experienced Andrew Griffiths, Australia's most successful author for small business, had other ideas. He convinced me that a business fiction style wasn't the most effective way to help build a practice. I accepted his advice and began a complete rewrite in a more normal business style.

This journey was assisted by my Accountability Group set up as part of the KPI program. My thanks to Jay McNabb, Adam Maher, Megan Tait, Peter Wilson and especially to Warwick Jackson.

As part of the rewrite of the book I began further research. In addition to reading every book and article and listening to every podcast I could find on customer success, I began a series of interviews with industry leaders. The following people were all kind enough to give me their time and input: Nick Bishara, Jeremy Goddard and Frank Volckmar, Objective Corporation; Will Bosma (who also arranged meetings with many of his contacts for me) and Brent Grimes, MuleSoft; Alan Frazer, ITT (who also arranged meetings for me); David Oakley, ServiceNow; Revathi Venkaratnam, Citrix; Greg Taylor, New Relic; Ashik Ahmed, Deputy; Matt Gurrie, Hansen Technologies; Ronnie Altit, Insentra; Stuart Geros, eMite; Robi Karp, Fluffy Spider; Ashley Ibrahim, Spectre Group; Matt Michaeliwicz, Complexica; Graham Pearson, Okta; Amit Bhandari, Mine Excellence; Lloyd Sheather, Demand Solutions; Paul Phillips, Manage Engine; Chris Donohoe, APIR; John Smith, Andor; Tuan Dao, Dialog; Nathan Lowe, ASI; Danie Blom, Accesstel; Vincent Fletcher, CartonCloud; Danielle Tricarico, PageUp People; Gordon Miles, ASTA Solutions; Mike Ryan, Vectra; Matt Larwood, AXIOS Development; Steve Bungay, Envision IT; Mike Capps, Redeye; Chloe Dervin, Webvine; Kareem Tawansi, Solentive; David Peters, Mahindra Comviva; Ben Leach, Hammertech; Adele Beachley, SOTI; Yathin Naidoo, Macromeasures; Todd Trevillian, Gruden; James Houston, Salesforce; Steve Ash, Think Procurement; Paul Keen, Airtasker; Steve Woodhouse, Land & Property Information (NSW Government); Daniel Pettman, Baptist Care; Martin McManus, DP World; Caroline Sweeney, Dimension Data; Jay Cao, QAD; Laurie Newman, PeopleMax.

Nick Maley spent lots of time guiding me on this second iteration of the book. Glenn Wright, Charles Summers, Mark Pretty and Tanya Graham also read various drafts and provided excellent guidance.

The book is deeply rooted in the experience of designing and running a customer success program across nine Asia-Pacific countries for more than five years. Lots of QADers contributed strongly to the program. My thanks go to Stefan deHaar, Jay Cao, Andrew Licence, Peace Chen, Clive Lovell, Jeremy Lai, Anton Chilton, Carter Lloyds, Gordon Fleming, Daniel Lender, Tanya Graham, Kaye Swanson, Yili Xu, Rob Jeremiassen, Kitty He, Prapan Potiratsombat, James Zhou, Andrew Lewin, Kylie Palmer, Frank Huang, Vijay Sabarwal, Jantima Kaenthaow, Sujoy Roychaudhury, Tony Armfield, Steve Moore and many others who had input to and implemented the program.

With the combined wisdom of the people I worked with, the people I interviewed and the people whose work I listened to and read, I wrote a first draft of this book.

About the Author

Paul has been an evangelist on outcomes for over a decade. And with outcomes as the theme, he's written two books and developed a program for each book.

Paul is now an author, speaker and consultant. Before this, he was the senior vice president of Asia-Pacific for an enterprise software company. He led 200 people in nine countries supporting 800 enterprise customers. His experience working across the region led to two insights on outcomes.

First, many organisations struggled to make their strategies work. He saw two problems. The organisations launched strategies without first developing execution capability. And they didn't coordinate implementation activities across departments. He realised a focus on internal outcomes would address these problems. He coined the phrase 'execution outcomes'. And wrote his first book, *The Chief Capability Officer – Delivering the Capability to Execute*. You can learn more about execution **capability** at www.coordinatedcapability.com.

The second insight—technology vendors weren't enabling outcomes the customers regarded as success. He decided his Asia Pacific team would do more to ensure the customers' success. So, he and his team pioneered an outcomes-based approach to customer engagement. They designed and ran the program across the entire Asia Pacific region. Paul and his team learnt what worked and what didn't work.

Having run the outcomes program for more than five years, he realised his experience could help other technology vendors. He also realised the nascent customer success movement provided a great vehicle for enabling these outcomes. He spent over a year researching customer success. He then blended that research and his own experience to develop the Generation 3 Customer Success program and write this book. You can learn more at www.gen3cs.com.

Bibliography

Adamson, B. D. (2015). *The Challenger Customer*. Penguin Group.

Brainyquotes. (n.d.). Marc Benioff Quotes. Retrieved from https://www.brainyquote.com/quotes/marc_benioff_5321 72

Covey, S. R. (1988). *The Seven Habits of Highly Effective People*. Free Press.

Dasteel, J. H. (2016). *Competing for Customers*. Pearson.

Dixon, M. a. (2011). *The Challenger Sale*. Penguin Group.

Dixon, M. T. (2013). *The Effortless Experience*. Penguin Group.

Duckworth, A. (2017). *Grit*. Vermilion.

Evans, B. (2017, July 26). 10 Powerful Examples of Microsoft CEO Satya Nadella's Transformative Vision. *Forbes*. Retrieved from https://www.forbes.com/sites/bobevans1/2017/07/26/1 0-powerful-examples-of-microsoft-ceo-satya-nadellas-transformative-vision/2/#6c1303cf48bf

Evans, B. (2017, August 28). Inside Salesforce.com's Customer Obsession: 10 Powerful Lessons From Marc Benioff. *Forbes*. Retrieved from https://www.forbes.com/sites/bobevans1/2017/08/28/in side-salesforce-coms-customer-obsession-10-powerful-lessons-from-marc-benioff/#2a042f3a1bbd

Evans, B. (2017, Nov 17). Why Salesforce.com, Workday And ServiceNow Are Obsessing Over This New Cloud Metric. *Forbes*. Retrieved from https://www.forbes.com/sites/bobevans1/2017/11/17/w hy-salesforce-com-workday-and-servicenow-are-obsessing-over-this-new-cloud-metric/#9628b1f22277

Hyken, S. (2016, December 3). How Effective Is Net Promoter Score (NPS)? *Forbes*. Retrieved from https://www.forbes.com/sites/shephyken/2016/12/03/ho w-effective-is-net-promoter-score-nps/#27de722423e4

Mehta, N. S. (2016). *Customer Success*. John Wiley & Sons.

Moore, G. A. (1991). *Crossing the Chasm*. Harper Business.

Planhat. (2017, August 28). Customer Success with Planhat.

Sturt, D. a. (2014, January 13). Delight Your Customers By Giving Them What They Didn't Ask For. *Forbes*. Retrieved from https://www.forbes.com/sites/davidsturt/2014/01/03/delight-your-customers-by-giving-them-what-they-didnt-ask-for/#51d6fc013ad5

Table of Figures

CPSIA information can be obtained
at www.ICGtesting.com
Printed in the USA
LVHW090727010620
656912LV00007B/885